D1224107

ORIENTAL RUGS

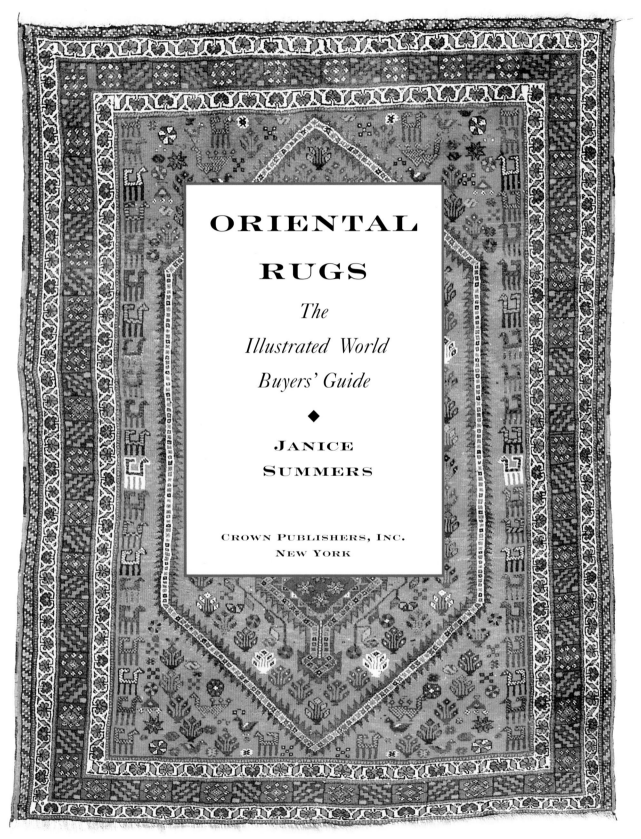

ORIENTAL RUGS

The

Illustrated World

Buyers' Guide

◆

JANICE
SUMMERS

CROWN PUBLISHERS, INC.
NEW YORK

NK
2808
.S88
1994

TO THE QASHQA'I WOMEN,

WHO SAID THEY WOULD TEACH ME THE IMPORTANT THINGS IN LIFE:

HOW TO SPIN, WEAVE, AND MAKE YOGURT BALLS.

◆

Copyright © 1994 by Janice Summers

All rights reserved. No part of this book may be reproduced or transmitted in any form
or by any means, electronic or mechanical, including photocopying, recording, or by any information storage and
retrieval system, without permission in writing from the publisher.

Published by Crown Publishers, Inc., 201 East 50th Street, New York, New York 10022.
Member of the Crown Publishing Group.

Random House, Inc. New York, Toronto, London, Sydney, Auckland.

CROWN is a trademark of Crown Publishers, Inc.

Manufactured in Hong Kong

Design by Linda Kocur

Maps and illustrations by Jason Küffer

Photographs by Jacques Bodenmann, Harold Bedoukian, Judith Cezar,
Jack Goldsmith, and Keith Marshall

Illustrations courtesy of Shimon Amir, Ararat Rug Company, Karabagh Carpets, Mori S.A., Roy Palmer,
Katherine Summers, Tola Carpets, Elie Watson, and Max Zollinger

Library of Congress Cataloging-in-Publication Data
Summers, Janice, 1945–
Oriental rugs: the illustrated world buyers' guide/by Janice Summers.
Includes bibliographical references and index.
1. Rugs, Oriental. I. Title.
NK2808.S88 1994
746.7'5'095075—dc20   93-21222 CIP

ISBN 0–517–59625–3
10 9 8 7 6 5 4 3 2 1
First Edition

LONGWOOD COLLEGE LIBRARY
FARMVILLE, VIRGINIA 23901

CONTENTS

Maps

PREFACE

Oriental Rugs: The Illustrated World Buyers' Guide is inspired by my love for Oriental carpets and my wish to convey an understanding and appreciation of the art of carpet weaving. I have written this book as a guide for anyone wanting to learn about Oriental rugs. In it I have explained how rugs are made, how to differentiate one rug from another, and how to care for them. New, used, and antique rugs are discussed and illustrated. The examples included represent rugs that are readily available in different markets around the world.

Rugs from the most important weaving centers are discussed and the most common designs are illustrated. Descriptions of structural characteristics, common designs, and color combinations are given. The text is supplemented with color illustrations of designs that are commonly woven in the village or town or by the tribe. Detailed photographs of the backs of the most important rugs aid in identification.

The rugs are grouped geographically, by country of origin or by region, as is the case with rugs of the Caucasus and Turkestan. The names of rugs used are those which are traditionally associated with them and are in common usage in the rug markets. Some of the names of places associated with rug weaving have changed over the years and are no longer found on maps. For example, Khotan is now known as Hotan or Hot'ien, yet antique rugs from this oasis are still known in the Oriental rug world as Khotan. Since this book is a buyer's guide, the names of towns and districts will be those used in the literature and the rug trade and not necessarily those found on current maps.

I gathered the information in this book on my recent field trips to the weaving centers. I am providing the most up-to-date information on the types of dyes currently used, changes in weaving practices, and new designs employed in the villages and towns and by the nomads. Drawing on my twenty-five years of experience in the Oriental rug business, I have given advice on what to look for and how to choose an Oriental rug. Also provided are tips on how to purchase a rug and how to maintain and care for it once it is in your home.

With this book I hope to stimulate your interest in and love of the Oriental rug art form. By looking at each rug, we can learn to appreciate the creativity of the designers and the skill of the weavers who put in hours and days individually tying knot after knot to produce a work of art for the floor. Sometimes the colors used may not be to our taste, but they reflect important aspects of the people and culture from which the rug comes. The more you learn about Oriental rugs, the more fun you can have with them. For anyone interested in more detailed information on specialized subjects, there are a number of good books available. I have included a list of recommended readings in the back of the book, where you will also find definitions of the special terms used in the book and summary charts of rug characteristics.

Half of the pleasure of owning an Oriental rug is buying it. Everyone remembers buying their first rug—how they haggled over the price or dragged it home. A rug is like a painting, only it is made for the floor. Rugs are meant to the enjoyed, walked on, talked about, and loved. Enjoy your search, and appreciate your rug.

ACKNOWLEDGMENTS

I would like to express my gratitude to many people who gave of their time and themselves to help in the preparation of this book:

Harold Bedoukian, Ararat Rug Company, Montreal; Gill Bennett and Keith Sulany, Tola Carpets, Montreal; Ali Afghahi, Kimiya Trading Co., Tehran, Iran; Jora Agha, Ersari Turkoman Project, Attock, Pakistan; Baz Mohammad, Turkmen Handicrafts, Islamabad, Pakistan; Lobsang Dorjee and Ngodup Lama, Culture Carpets, Kathmandu, Nepal; Jeanne Fredericks, Susan Urstadt, New Canaan, Conn.; Dimitru Oancea and Tania Miclea, ICECOOP S.A., Bucharest, Romania; Chris Walter, Yayla Tribal Rugs, Cambridge, Mass.; Reza Zollanvari, Zollanvari, Zurich, Switzerland; Gholam Reza Zollanvari and Ali Parto, Zollanvari, Shiraz, Iran.

To Harold Bedoukian, a very special thank-you for all of your encouragement and professional advice in addition to your help with supplying the illustrations and maps used in this book. My deepest appreciation to my friends Gill Bennett and Lily Hechtman for their encouragement and advice and to Jack Goldsmith, Judith Cezar, and Keith Marshall for their photography. Many thanks to Chris Bedoukian, Kevin Marpole, Richard Lelievre, Francis Lelievre, Aleric Pitt, Nashaat Zamzam, Tim Seah, and Pierette Casault for all their hard work. To my editor Sharon Squibb and everyone at Crown who made this book possible, my heartfelt thanks to all of you.

GARRUS CARPET, 8' x 18'

one

WHAT IS AN ORIENTAL RUG?

n authentic Oriental rug is a handmade carpet that is either knotted with pile or woven without pile. Traditionally, Oriental rugs have been woven in Iran, Turkey, Pakistan, India, Afghanistan, China, the Caucasus (currently the republics of Armenia and Azerbaijan and the Autonomous Republic of Daghestan), and Turkestan (Republic of Turkmenistan). Oriental-design rugs made by machine or any method other than handknotting or handweaving do not qualify as genuine Oriental rugs.

Many different cultures, religious affiliations, and ethnic groups are responsible for weaving Oriental carpets; Buddhists, Christians, Hindus, Jews, Muslims, as well as adherents of other religions have been involved in carpet weaving. In some carpets, religious symbols are evident in the designs and motifs used.

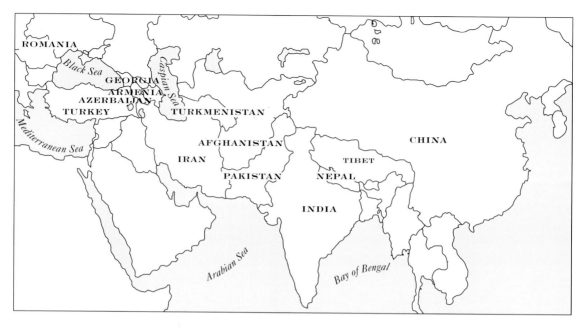

MAJOR ORIENTAL RUG-WEAVING COUNTRIES

The designs and variations used in Oriental rugs are so numerous that it would be impossible to describe them all. Interestingly, many of the designs used in Oriental rugs are also seen in other art forms such as textiles, sculpture, ceramics, tiles, and frescoes.

A common misconception is that "no two Oriental rugs are the same." Although this is true in essence, the implication needs to be further qualified. Since each rug is handmade, slight variations in weave and design are inevitable. And no matter how skilled the weaver is, it is impossible to exactly duplicate another rug; every rug will differ.

Although the Oriental rug marketplace is constantly changing in the variety and the types of carpets available, the weaving process has remained unchanged over the centuries. Historically, the weaving of Oriental rugs and the designs woven in them have been affected by political disputes, wars, and political instability and upheavals as well as by industrial development, laws, and embargoes over political differences. For example, the U.S. embargo on Iranian goods since 1987 has increased the production of Persian design rugs in China, Pakistan, India, and Romania. During the 1980–89 war in Afghanistan, rugs were woven with guns, tanks, helicopters, and other military motifs.

Many rugs of excellent quality are being handwoven today. Their designs are well executed and their color combinations are very pleasing. Oriental rugs are available in surprisingly broad ranges of colors and designs to fit any decor and lifestyle. In some countries, such as India, Pakistan, and China, carpet weaving has evolved into a mass-produced commercial activity.

Program lines have been developed consisting of rugs of a specific design woven in a variety of color combinations and sizes. In other areas, tribal women still spin and dye their own wool. The dyes are gathered locally from shrubs, roots, and trees. These women do not use cartoons or pieces of paper to tell them what to weave, but rather they weave what they feel and see around them. The different circumstances under which a rug is made, whether in a large factory, a small workshop, an individual home, or by a nomad, are reflected in the designs and materials used. In the following chapters rugs woven under all these conditions are discussed. From this information it is my hope that an understanding and love of this handwoven art form will be gained.

WEAVING A "TIBETAN" RUG IN NEPAL

A YOUNG WOMAN AT HER LOOM IN ISFAHAN, IRAN

two

RUG CONSTRUCTION

riental pile rugs are hand-knotted on a foundation formed by warp and weft threads. Hand-knotted carpets are composed of three parts: warp, weft, and pile. During the weaving process the *warp* threads are attached to the upper and lower beams of the loom. They run vertically through the body of the carpet. A strand of wool is looped around a pair of warp threads, forming a knot. The loose ends of the knots make up the body of the carpet and are called the *pile*. *Weft* threads run horizontally through the carpet and are used to secure the rows of knots in place.

The weaving process is done on a loom or a frame upon which warp threads have been attached. A strand of yarn is looped around a pair of warps and cut. The process is repeated across the width of a carpet. After a row of knots has been completed, one weft is passed over alternate warps. If a second weft is used, it is passed under the same warps, reversing the sequence. Consecutive wefts would follow this same pattern. After the designated number of wefts are passed, the wefts and knots are beaten firmly with a heavy "comb." This process is repeated row after row until the carpet has been completed.

The designs are formed by the arrangement of different-colored knotted yarns. The placement of each knot is directed by following a *cartoon*, by having a master weaver chant the design pattern, or from memory. A design is usually drawn to scale on a grid paper, with each square representing a single knot. The design is then painted and cut into strips. These strips are either encased in plastic or mounted on a board and varnished, to protect them for future years of use.

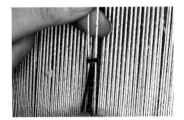

TYING A SYMMETRICAL
KNOT

LOOMS

◆

There are two basic types of looms: the *horizontal* or ground loom and the *vertical* or upright loom. There are three variations of the vertical loom: the village type, Tabriz type, and roller beam type.

The horizontal loom is used primarily by nomads, some seminomadic tribes, and some villagers. Looms of this type are easily collapsed and moved during migration. The warps are attached to the upper and lower beams, which are held in place by large stakes driven into the ground. It is much more difficult to maintain an even warp tension with this type of loom, and rugs woven on horizontal looms frequently have irregular sides. Horizontal looms are usually set up outside or under a tent and one or more weavers sit on the completed part of the carpet as work progresses up the loom.

TYPES OF COMBS USED
IN WEAVING

BAKHTIARI WEAVER
AT HER LOOM IN
SHAHR-E-KORD

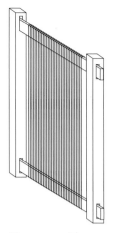

VILLAGE LOOM

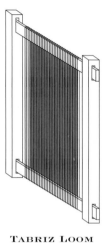

TABRIZ LOOM

CARTOON FOR A PANEL DESIGN BAKHTIARI CARPET

ROLLER BEAM LOOM

The *village* type is the simplest of the vertical looms. The weaver sits on a plank which is raised as the weaving progresses, enabling the weaver to sit directly in front of the area of the carpet on which he or she is working. The warp threads are attached to the upper and lower beams. The length of the carpet is usually as long as the distance between the upper and lower beams. It is possible to make the carpet longer by loosening the warp threads and reattaching the completed part of the carpet to the lower beam.

The *Tabriz* loom is slightly more complicated than the village type. The warp threads pass in a continuous loop around the upper and lower beams. Warp tension is maintained by driving wedges in the space where the side supports meet the lower beam. The weavers do not have to be raised with this type of loom; as the weaving progresses, the rug is lowered down around the lower beam and up the back of the loom. The completed part of the carpet can easily be inspected. With this type of loom the carpet can be as long as twice the distance between the upper and lower beams.

The *roller beam* type is a rather sophisticated loom. The

warp and weft threads are wound around the upper beam, leaving the ends attached to the lower beam. As the weaving progresses, the warp threads are unwound from the upper beam and the finished part of the carpet is rolled around the lower beam. It is easy to weave carpets of any length on this type of loom. The warp tension is easily maintained by levers which adjust and rotate the beams.

SHEARING,
CARDING, AND
COMBING
◆

Sheep whose wool is to be used for carpet making are shorn in the spring and fall. The wool is then thoroughly washed to remove dirt, grease, and any other impurities that may have accumulated, then it is dried and sorted.

The wool is then combed. The fibers are aligned so that they all lie in the same direction, and when spun will produce a strong yarn. Combing also removes any impurities that may be left in the wool and separates the long from the short fibers. It is done with a piece of wood with several rows of nails or metal teeth at one end, called a comb. The wool is pulled through the teeth; then it is reversed and pulled back through the teeth again.

Carding is the process that prepares the wool for spinning. It is done with two wooden paddles, called *cards*, which contain metal teeth that slant slightly toward the handle. A batch of wool is placed on one of the paddles and the second paddle is passed through the first. This is done several times until the fibers of the wool are entangled and it becomes soft and fuzzy. The wool can then be removed from the card in even layers and is ready to be spun.

SPINNING
◆

TYPES OF SPINDLES USED
IN HAND-SPINNING

The drawing out and twisting of fibers together into a strand of yarn is called *spinning*. This process can be done either by hand or machine. Wool fibers are spun together to form a strand of yarn. Two or more strands of wool are twisted together to form *plied* yarn.

Hand-spinning is done with the use of a *spindle*, which is composed of a wooden dowel and a crosspiece or disk. The spinner will pull out the fibers, twist them together, attach them to the spindle, and give the spindle a twist. The spindle is fed by loose fibers that are wrapped around the wrist or arm of the spinner. Spinning is also done with a spinning wheel on which

a spindle is attached; a rotating wheel adjusts the yarn.

The direction that the yarn is twisted is either clockwise in a right-hand direction, called *S-spun*, or counterclockwise in a left-hand direction, called *Z-spun*. The same terminology is used for the plying of the yarns, *S-plied* or *Z-plied*. The strands are plied in the opposite direction than they are spun. For example, a warp thread that consists of three strands of S-spun wool that have been Z-plied would be written "S3Z."

WARP

◆

Z-SPUN

During the weaving process the warps are attached to the upper and lower beams of the loom. After the weaving is completed and the carpet is removed from the loom, the loose warp threads are called the *fringe*.

A knot is formed as a strand of wool is looped around a pair of warp threads. The warp threads run vertically through the body of the carpet. The material used for the warp threads must be strong and the warps must be tightly strung on the loom, with an even tension. Uneven warp tension will result in bumps or ridges in the carpet.

Fibers. Cotton, wool, and silk are the primary materials used for the warp threads. Goat's hair is used occasionally by tribal weavers. The type, thickness, and color of warp fibers vary from village to village and tribe to tribe. These differences will be discussed later under individual rug types.

Cotton used for warps is spun either by machine or by hand. Machine-spun cotton warps were introduced in the rug-weaving industry as early as the mid-19th century. Most of the early machine-spun warps used in Oriental rugs were of Indian cotton that was spun in England. Machine-spun warps are uniform strands, generally of five or more ply. Hand-spun warps usually are more coarsely spun and are less uniform in appearance. Hand-spun cotton warps are used in three or four plies, but rarely more than five.

Silk is the thinnest of the natural fibers used for warp threads. It is the strongest in relationship to its diameter and has the greatest tensile strength. Some of the most finely knotted carpets are woven with silk warps.

Wool used for the warp threads is spun either by hand or machine, then plied. The number of plies varies according to

A BAKHTIARI WOMAN
HAND-SPINNING WOOL
WITH A DROP SPINDLE

the weaving center. Undyed wool is generally used for warps; variances in color are due to the different breeds of sheep.

Goat's hair is occasionally mixed with wool for warps and wefts by some tribal weavers. It is blended into the wool during the carding or combing process.

Warp Level. Warp threads may lie on the same level or be depressed (offset onto different levels). The degree of warp depression depends largely on how tightly the weft thread is pulled. Rugs with warps on the same level have wefts woven through the warps. Rugs woven with warp threads on different levels have at least one weft shoot that is tightly pulled. If a second weft is used, it is loosely woven through the warps. Consecutive even and odd wefts would follow this pattern.

When viewed from the back, rugs with warp threads on the same level have both nodes (the looped portion) of the knot equally visible, side by side; in those with warps on different levels, one node is compressed deeper to some degree into the foundation, behind the other node. The degree of depression can result in a ridged appearance on the back of the rug. These ridges vary depending on the degree of depression. The degree of warp depression is one of the factors that affect the knot count of a rug.

SYMMETRICAL KNOT WITH WARPS ON THE SAME LEVEL

SYMMETRICAL KNOT WITH WARPS ON DIFFERENT LEVELS

WEFT
◆

The weft threads run horizontally through the carpet and are used to secure the knots in place. A pass of a single weft between two rows of knots is called a *shoot*.

The number of shoots used between knot rows varies depending on the weaver and the weaving area. In some rugs there may be as many as four or more weft shoots between the rows of knots. These variations will also be discussed later with the individual rug types.

Cotton, wool, silk, and goat's hair are the most frequently used fibers for wefts. Wefts can also appear in combinations of wool and cotton as well as a blend of wool and goat's hair. For example, a rug with three shoots of wefts may have one of wool and two of cotton; or a rug may have two shoots of wool and goat's hair that have been plied together.

Cotton wefts are spun by hand or machine. They may be undyed or dyed in a variety of colors, such as red, pink, light blue, or dark blue. Wool wefts are also spun either by hand or machine. They may be used in their natural color, such as ivory, dark brown, gray, or black, or dyed red or blue. Silk wefts may be dyed or undyed. Goat's hair is used in its natural undyed state, usually dark brown or black.

PILE
♦

The pile of a rug is composed of the loose cut ends of the knots. The majority of carpets are woven with wool pile. Wools vary greatly from region to region. Many different factors affect the texture, color, and quality of the wool used for the pile.

Kork wool is used for the pile of the finer-quality Iranian rugs from Qum, Kashan, Isfahan, and Nain. This wool comes from the underwool of the sheep from the spring shearing.

"Skin" or "dead" wool is removed from butchered sheep rather than being sheared. The animal skin is subjected to a caustic solution to facilitate the removal of the wool from the skin. This wool has a dry, bristly feel and is very brittle.

Silk may be used for the entire pile or in small amounts to accentuate certain designs and motifs. Because of its expense, the majority of silk pile carpets are woven in small sizes.

Mercerized cotton or artificial silk resembles silk and is occasionally sold to the unsuspecting buyer as silk. The use of artificial silk is common in Turkish Kayseri and some Indian and Turkoman rugs.

Camel's hair is used for the pile in some Kurdish rugs and Balouchi rugs. It has a different feel than sheep's wool and possesses a distinctive odor when wet.

Goat's hair is occasionally used for the pile by some Balouchi weavers for design accents. It is used undyed and has a bristly feel.

Cotton is occasionally used in the pile, in small amounts as a decorative accent, in some Turkish and Turkoman rugs. White cotton is much brighter than white wool and does not have the lustrous appearance of wool.

There are two different methods for attaching the spun yarn to the warp threads: the *symmetrical* or the *asymmetrical* knot. These terms describe how the yarn appears attached to the warps.

In older Oriental rug literature the *symmetrical* knot is referred to as the Turkish or Ghiordes knot and the *asymmetrical* knot as the Persian or Senna knot. This manner of naming the knots after towns or countries where the knot may or may not have been used was misleading and confusing. For example, the so-called Senna knot was not woven in Senna.

The *symmetrical* knot is formed by a strand of yarn which completely encircles two warp threads; the loose ends then are drawn tightly between these two warps and cut.

The *asymmetrical* knot is formed as a strand of yarn encircles one warp thread and winds around the other. One loose end is pulled through the two warps; the other emerges outside of the paired warps either to the left or right side.

The *jufti* or "double" knot is simply the symmetrical or asymmetrical knot tied around four warp threads instead of two. This manner of knotting allows the weaver to tie half the number of knots that would be normally required. The density of the pile is also half the normal amount.

To identify the type of knot used, bend the rug horizontally and open the pile. The symmetrical knot is the easiest to identify as the strand of encircling yarn is visible as it passes over the two warps.

To remove the finished carpet from the loom, the warps must be cut. The portion of the cut warps attached to the carpet is called the *fringe*. The cut warps or fringe must be finished in a way that prevents the loss of knots.

The most common methods used to finish the ends of a rug are to use either a knotted fringe or a narrow kelim with fringe. A *kelim* is a flat woven strip formed by weaving the wefts back and forth through the warps. The kelim may be plain or woven in different-colored stripes, or decorated with small embroidered or knotted-pile motifs or with a single line of two intertwining yarns. Some rugs have fringe at one end only. The other end may have warps that are braided, turned under, and sewn to the back of the carpet, or a small finished band of kelim.

PLAIN COTTON FRINGE
(TABRIZ)

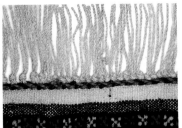

KELIM WITH KNOTTED
WOOL FRINGE (BALOUCHI)

SOUMAK STITCH WITH ROWS
OF KNOTS (KUBA)

SIDE
FINISHES
◆

The sides of an Oriental carpet may be secured and reinforced in several different ways. With one method, a single terminal warp or a cord formed of several terminal warps is wrapped with the weft threads, forming an edge called the *selvedge*. The selvedge may be reinforced by an additional *overcasting* of wool, cotton, silk, or goat's hair.

Overcasting is usually done with one color of yarn along the entire side of the carpet. The sides of some rugs are decorated with two colors of yarn, yielding a striped overcasting or multicolored bands along the sides of the rug. Another way is with double-cord side finishing; two terminal warps or two bundles of terminal warps are wrapped by the wefts in a figure-eight stitch. This type of finishing also may be reinforced by an additional overcasting. Three- and four-cord side finishings follow the same pattern.

In some areas the terminal warp threads are not wrapped by the wefts during the weaving process. Instead, the side cord is added after the carpet has been completed and removed from the loom. A single cord is then sewn onto the side of the carpet and overcast, usually with wool.

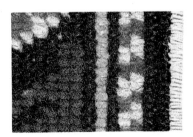

SINGLE CORD WRAPPED
WITH COTTON WEFTS (KHILA)

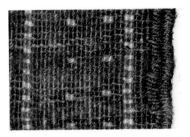

DOUBLE CORD OVERCAST
WITH WOOL (KUBA)

TRIPLE CORD OVERCAST
WITH WOOL (GENDGE)

QASHQA'I WOMAN DYEING WOOL

three

NATURAL AND SYNTHETIC DYES

he dyeing of wool is a delicate process which varies according to the dyestuff used and the color desired. Commercially this process is directed by a master dyer, who is a highly skilled and respected craftsman in a profession that demands accuracy as well as skill.

Before dyeing, all excess oils and grease must be removed from the wool so that the dye can penetrate the fibers. The wool is then treated with a mordant to facilitate the adherence of the dye to the fibers. (An exception, to be described later, is wool to be dyed with indigo.)

A *mordant* is a metallic salt which enables the dye to affix itself to the wool fibers, thus improving the colorfastness of the dye. The mordant binds to the wool fiber and the dye then binds to the mordanted wool. The mordants most commonly used are alum, iron, chrome, and

25

tin. The mordant used can affect the color or tint obtained; for example, tin mordants tend to brighten colors and iron mordants tend to darken them.

The dye is dissolved in water, called the dyebath. The wool, in skeins (loosely coiled lengths), is submerged in the dyebath, which is heated and brought to a boil. The wool is stirred through the dyebath to ensure uniform dyeing. After the dyeing has been completed, the wool is hung in the sun to dry. It must be turned periodically to prevent the color from collecting at the bottom of the skeins.

Dyeing with indigo is different from that using other dyestuffs. Indigo is not soluble in water and must be dissolved in an alkaline solution, through fermentation. Wool is soaked and squeezed before entering the vat to ensure that no air will be introduced into the dyebath. Care is also taken to slide the wool down the side of the dyebath to prevent air from entering. Air in the dyebath will cause uneven dyeing. When the wool is removed from the vat and exposed to air, it gradually turns blue through reoxidation and the dye is fixed to the wool. Repeating this process darkens the wool.*

There are two types of dyes used in the dyeing of wool: natural dyestuffs and synthetic dyes. Natural dyestuffs are those which are derived from either a vegetable or animal source. Vegetable sources can be a plant, root, flower, seed, or fruit. There are different types of *synthetic dyes*: direct dyes (acid or basic), mordant dyes, and fiber-reacting dyes.

NATURAL
DYESTUFFS
◆

Madder. Red dye extracted from the root of the madder plant (*Rubia tinctorum*). Madder is cultivated throughout the Middle East and Asia. The color of the red obtained varies depending on the mordant used; for example, wool dyed with madder and an alum mordant yields a rich red, an iron mordant yields purple, a tin mordant yields orange, and a chrome mordant yields a brownish-red color.

Cochineal. Red dye extracted from the female cochineal insect (*Dactylopius coccus cacti*). The insects are collected from

*Harold Bedoukian, "Natural Dyes in Caucasian Rugs," *Oriental Rug Review* II: 7 (October 1982), 25–26.

cactus plants in Central and South America, killed in boiling water, then dried. The dyestuff is extracted by boiling or steaming the dried bodies. Cochineal with an alum mordant yields a dull red, a tin mordant bright red, a chrome mordant purple, and an iron mordant gray.

Lac. Red dye derived from a resinous substance secreted by a shelled insect (*Coccus lacca*) indigenous to India and Southeast Asia. The insects deposit the substance on twigs while feeding. The twigs are then collected and boiled to extract the dye. With an alum mordant, lac yields a scarlet red.

Kermes. Red dye extracted from the bodies of an insect (*Kermes ilicis*), found in the bark of evergreen oak bushes around Mount Ararat. The insects were collected and treated in much the same way as cochineal. The dye is known in Armenian literature as *vortan garmir*, which means worm red. The color obtained varies according to the mordant used. A tin mordant yields orange, iron purple, and alum red.

Indigo. Blue dye extracted from the leaves of the indigo plant (*Indigo tinctoria*). It is widely cultivated throughout the Orient, with the best quality coming from India. Wool to be dyed indigo does not need to be treated with a mordant before the dyebath. And since indigo seems to make wool more resilient, indigo-dyed wool pile will be slightly longer than surrounding wool of a different color after years of wear.

Weld. Yellow dye extracted from all parts of the weld plant (*Reseda luteola*), especially the tops of the flowers. Weld is an excellent dye source as it does not fade with age. With an alum mordant, weld yields a saturated bright yellow color, with chrome mordant an olive yellow, and with tin mordant a yellow olive.

Saffron. Yellow dye extracted from the dried stigmas of the saffron flower (*Crocus sativus*). The plant is indigenous to the Orient and was grown in Turkey and Iran.

Pomegranate. Yellow dye extracted from the fruit of the pomegranate tree (*Punica granatum*). Pomegranate rind with an alum mordant yields a yellow color, but with an iron mordant the color is black.

Onion. Yellow dye extracted from the membranes (skins) of the onion bulb (*Allium cepa*). Onion skins with an alum mordant yield a golden yellow, with chrome a copper color.

Walnut. Brown dye extracted from the green husks of the walnut tree (*Juglans regia*). It is not necessary to use previously mordanted wool when dyeing with walnut husks. However, if wool mordanted with an alum is used, a dark-brown color is obtained, and chrome-mordanted wool will produce a light-brown (khaki) color.

Oak. Bark, galls, and acorn cups from the oak tree (*Quercus macrolepis* and other species) are used with an iron mordant to dye wool black. The use of the mordant caused oxidation, resulting in corrosion of the wool. An alum-mordant oak bark is used to produce a yellowish tan and a chrome-mordant a dark-yellow tan.

OVERDYEING
◆

Certain colors are obtained by overdyeing one dyestuff with another. For example, green is obtained by vat-dyeing with indigo and overdyeing with a yellow dyestuff. Overdyeing indigo with madder yields a purple color.

Other colors can be obtained by mixing two different dyestuffs in the same dyebath. Orange is obtained by adding madder plus a yellow dyestuff to the same dyebath.

SYNTHETIC DYES
◆

The first synthetic dye, discovered in London in 1856 by William Henry Perkins, was an aniline dye, a derivative of coal tar. Synthetic dyes were available commercially by the 1870s and soon began to replace natural dyes because they were easier and cheaper to use. Unfortunately these dyes were not colorfast.

Aniline dyes are *direct basic dyes*. They are applied directly to the wool in an alkaline solution. The first aniline dye, known as "mauveine" or "aniline purple," was not colorfast. It was sensitive to light and with time faded into a brownish-gray color. Other aniline dyes were also produced in blue, green, and violet.

Direct acid dyes, introduced in the 1870s, were applied to the wool in an acidic dyebath. These dyes did not fade when exposed to sunlight; however, they did bleed when wet. The colors obtained from these dyes were often harsh. A variety of acid dyes were used during the late 19th and early 20th centuries, with names like Ponceau 2R (Russian Red), Rocceline, Orange II, and Croceine Orange.

Azo dyes, a type of direct acid dye, were introduced during

THE RED ANILINE DYE HAS FADED ON THE TOP OF THE RUG. ON THE BACK, THE ORIGINAL COLOR HAS REMAINED. THE BLUE DYE IS INDIGO.

SENNA KELIM WITH
ABRASH, 4' X 6'

the last quarter of the 19th century. Depending on the color, some were more susceptible to bleeding than others.

In the 1940s, *chrome dyes*, which use a chromium mordant, were developed. The wool is treated with potassium dichromate so that it will take the dye more readily and evenly. With chrome dyes this can be done before, during, or after the dyebath. Chrome dyes are colorfast.

Dyes that combine the dyestuff and the mordant into one dye are known as *metal complex dyes*.

Fiber-reacting dyes are those in which the dye chromogen, the color-giving part of the dye molecule, chemically binds with the wool molecule to form a new molecule, thus becoming part of its chemical structure. Dyes of this type are very colorfast. Fiber-reacting dyes were discovered in 1956 and are more expensive to use.

ABRASH
◆

In some carpets, a slight variation in tone or hue may be visible within one color area. This is called an *abrash*. These slight changes of color occur either because of the uneven absorption of the dye by the yarn or as a result of the use of wool from different dye lots. Many different factors can affect the uniform absorption of the dye, for example, air in the dyebath, impurities in the wool, or uneven thickness of the yarn. Wool of two different dye lots is evident by horizontal bands or lines of different shades across the width of a carpet.

WASHES
◆

Most Oriental rugs are washed before being exported to remove dust, excess wool, and any dirt that may have accumulated on the surface during the weaving process. The washing may be done in streams, weaving establishments, or large specialized washing factories. After washing, the carpets are spread in the sun to dry. Because the sun in the rug-making areas is so intense, it also softens the colors.

Chemical Wash. A light chemical wash is given to many Oriental rugs to soften their colors. This does not harm or affect the durability of the carpet. The type of wool used and the chemical concentration of the wash affect the degree to which the colors are toned down.

Luster Wash. A luster, or sheen, may be given to a carpet by

PERSIAN RUGS BEING WASHED BEFORE EXPORT FROM REY

a chemical wash. Certain wools are more receptive to the process than others, and gain a more lustrous appearance.

Antique Wash. To give an aged or old look to carpets, an "antique" or chemical wash was developed to tone down the colors. This process bleaches the color from the tips of the pile and gives it a drab, muted appearance. Some antique washes give a brownish cast to the pile and fringes. The practice can easily be detected by folding the rug and examining the base of the pile. The tips of the pile will appear much lighter than the base.

"PAINTED" RUGS

◆

During the 1920s and '30s, many rugs exported from Iran were thought to be too bright for the American market and were given a chemical wash to tone down the colors. The washing tended to reduce brilliant red background colors to a drab, muted pinkish rose, and since a darker maroon red was more appealing to American tastes, a "painting" process was initiated. In New York, the background color was dyed the darker maroon with the use of a hand-applied dye. Another process was then necessary to add the desired luster or sheen to the rug. Almost all Sarouks as well as some Dergazines, Mahals, Lillihans, Isfahans, and Hamadans imported during this period were both washed and painted. The value of these rugs was not affected by having been painted; however, if the paint was not evenly applied, resulting in a blotchy appearance, the value would be less.

The term "painted" is also used to refer to rugs with worn areas that have been colored by ink, felt-tip pens, or acrylic paints. After years of use, some rugs develop unsightly worn spots in areas where there was traffic. The light-colored warps and wefts that clearly show through the thin or worn-off darker-colored wool pile can then be camouflaged by painting or "spot-dyeing" them the same color as the pile. A worn rug that has been painted will be less valuable than a comparable rug in good condition.

CARPETS LAID IN THE SUN TO DRY AFTER BEING WASHED

CURVILINEAR MEDALLION DESIGN (MERIGEH), 3' x 5'

four

ELEMENTS OF DESIGN

riental rug designs are of two basic types: rectilinear and curvilinear. Rectilinear designs are composed of angular, geometric motifs and patterns. Curvilinear designs consist of floral, flowing motifs and patterns and tend to be more intricate and refined than rectilinear designs. Some rugs contain a combination of both curvilinear and rectilinear designs.

By design, an Oriental rug can be divided into two parts: the field and the border. The field is the center and focal point of the rug; the border serves as a frame for the design used in the field. The field composition can be classified into seven basic types: medallion, repeated motif, allover pattern, empty or open field, compartmentalized or panel, picture or portrait, and prayer. Each of these design types has numerous variations.

MEDALLION

◆

A medallion design rug has a field which is dominated by a single central medallion or by two or more medallions. The central medallion often appears with quarter medallions in the corners of the field, called *spandrels*. In Persian the medallion-and-corner-design combination is called *lechek torunj*.

Medallions appear in many different styles, sizes, and shapes: multilobed, geometric, floral, elongated, or even animal. The field surrounding the medallion may be open (empty), semiopen (a few motifs in the field), or filled. A central medallion may be superimposed on a field that is filled with a repeated motif or an overall pattern.

REPEATED MOTIF

◆

Rugs woven with a repeated motif have a field that is filled with multiple rows of the same motif or design element. This type of design is often used in conjunction with a central medallion. The Boteh, Herati, Zil-i-Sultan, Mina Khani, Gul-i-Henna, and Gul motifs are most often used as repeating patterns.

ALLOVER PATTERN

◆

The allover pattern has a field which is filled with a variety of motifs that have neither a repeated nor a regimented form. In some instances, the pattern is large in scale and fills the field.

RECTILINEAR MEDALLION (GOLTUK),
4' x 6'6"

REPEATED MOTIF (BALOUCHI),
4' x 6'4"

ALLOVER PATTERN (QUM),
4' x 6'

Several types of patterns which can be grouped with this type of design are the Shah Abbas, Hunting, and Vase or Tree patterns.

The Shah Abbas pattern, named after the patron of the Persian carpet industry, fills the field with palmettes and flowers interspersed within an intricate network of vines and tendrils. This type of design contains very little repetition and is quite often used in conjunction with a central medallion and spandrels.

A Vase or Tree pattern has either a vase or a tree in the center of the base of the field. From this tree or vase emanate tendrils or branches with florals, leaves, or vines that expand to fill the field. The Tree-of-Life and Weeping Willow are examples of the Tree pattern. Vase motifs are most frequently woven in Kashan.

Hunting or Garden design rugs are woven with combinations of trees, flowers, animals, birds, and human figures in a nature scene. The Hunting design is a variation of the Garden pattern in which one or more hunters are depicted, often on horseback with bows and arrows. This Hunting design is associated with the Persian weaving center of Tabriz and copies of Tabriz rugs woven in India, Pakistan, and Romania.

OPEN FIELD

◆

Open field rugs have no motifs or design elements in the field of the rug. An empty field is surrounded by a series of borders, which contain a variety of motifs reflecting the origin of the rug. Some carpets woven with no field pattern have an elaborate series of borders. Rugs with an open field have been woven in Talish, Kazak, Tibet, Nepal, Oushak, and Sultanabad.

COMPART-MENTALIZED (PANEL)

◆

The field of a carpet with a compartmentalized design is divided into square, rectangular, onion-dome, or diamond-shaped compartments. Lattice and Trellis patterns may also be included with this type of design. The compartments or panels enclose a variety of motifs: flowers, trees, boteh, stars, palmettes, and small geometric figures.

The panel design is derived from the matrix formed by irrigation channels in Persian gardens. Designs of this type were woven as early as the 17th century. The panels can be arranged by color or design, or randomly.

OPEN FIELD (TIBETAN),
6' x 9'

COMPARTMENTALIZED OR PANEL
(BAKHTIARI), 4'6" x 6'6"

PICTURE
(PORTRAIT)

◆

PICTURE (BALOUCHI),
3' x 5'

Pictorial carpets, influenced by European oil paintings, prints, and later by photography, began to appear in the late 18th century. Carpets with idyllic landscapes, scenes of bazaars, historic monuments, battlefield victories, and copies of famous European paintings are woven. Scenes from the poems of Omar Khayyam, and from the traditional love stories of Khosrow, Shirin, and Farhad as well as Leyli and Majnun are popular designs seen in Persian carpets.

Portrait carpets attempt to realistically portray a specific person or persons: heroes, poets, political and religious leaders. In Persian rugs, shahs, kings, khans, presidents, and tsars have been depicted. In Turkish carpets, Ataturk, the father of modern Turkey, was a favorite subject. Portraits of Lenin were woven in some Caucasian and Turkoman rugs. Portrait carpets woven in the urban centers are finely woven with features of a specific person recognizable. In nomadic carpets, the interpretation of a person or group of people is more abstract.

In 1980, Afghan and Balouchi rugs first appeared with weapons of war—Kalashnikov rifles, grenades, tanks, helicopters, and airplanes—depicted in their fields.

Prayer rugs have a prayer niche (*mihrab*) or arch at the top of the field. The arch may be either geometric or curvilinear, depending on where the rug was woven. In some weaving centers, the prayer arch is supported by a single or double pair of columns. The area on either side of the prayer arch is known as a spandrel. These areas are decorated in a variety of different patterns according to the weaving center. Turkish prayer rugs often have a panel either at the top or bottom of the field.

The field of a prayer rug may be empty or filled with design elements common to the area. A Marasali prayer rug, for example, has a rectilinear prayer arch with a field that is filled with rows of multicolored geometric boteh. Prayer rugs are woven throughout Turkey, Iran, Afghanistan, the Caucasus, and Turkestan. Copies of traditional Persian and Turkish patterns are woven in Pakistan, India, China, and Romania.

Rugs with multiple mihrabs arranged side by side are referred to as *saffs*. The fields of the mihrabs are empty or filled with a vase or tree. Saffs are woven in eastern Turkestan and in Turkey. Copies of Turkish saffs are woven in Pakistan.

PRAYER RUG (KIRSEHIR),
3'5" x 6'

BOTEH (PAISLEY) The boteh, or paisley, motif is used by Persian, Caucasian, Turkoman, Indian, Turkish, and Pakistani weavers. The motif appears in both curvilinear and rectilinear forms, as well as in many different sizes and shapes, and is used in the field as well as the borders. As a field motif, it is repeated in rows, diagonal stripes, or vertical columns. It is also used as a filler inside medallions and spandrels or as the background motif of a rug. On rare occasions, the boteh may be used as a central medallion figure.

HERATI The Herati (*Mahi*) motif consists of a rosette urrounded by four lancet-shaped leaves or "fish." The majority of weaving centers used the rosette within a diamond shape or lozenge; however, some rugs from the Khorasan province are woven without the diamond shape surrounding the rosette.

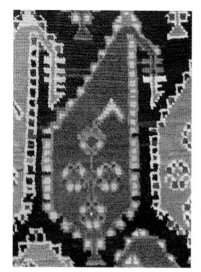

BOTEH

HERATI

ZIL-I-SULTAN

ZIL-I-SULTAN The Zil-i-Sultan design is composed of repeated rows of vases of roses. Spaces between the vases occasionally are filled with flowers or by confronting birds. This design is used primarily in the Persian weaving centers of Tabriz and Abadeh, and also among the Afshar and Qashqa'i tribes.

MINA KHANI The Mina Khani pattern is composed of repeated floral motifs, each surrounded by four similar, smaller flowers that are joined in turn by vines to form a diamond arrangement. This design is found in older Bijars, Hamadans, and Kurds and the majority of carpets woven in Veramin.

GUL-I-HENNA The Gul-i-Henna (henna flower) design is composed of rows of small plantlike motifs that resemble stalks with flowers and leaves. These motifs are contained within a diamond-shaped bouquet. This pattern is used in older rugs from the Hamadan and Sultanabad areas.

GUL-I-FRANC The Gul-i-Franc (French flower) motif consists of an arrangement of rather large, cabbagelike roses. These bouquets are repeated in rows throughout the field. This type of design was used in Bijar and Senna as well as in the Bakhtiari villages of the Chahar Mahal.

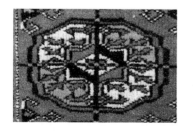

GUL

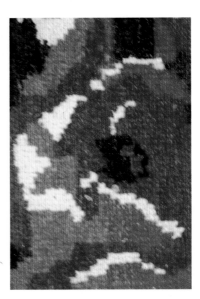

MINA KHANI   GUL-I-HENNA   GUL-I-FRANC

MEMLING GUL

GUL The Gul (Persian for flower) is a small rectilinear motif that was once unique to the Turkoman tribe that wove it. In addition to the basic guls there are numerous variations of each. Guls are repeated in rows throughout the field. Turkoman rugs are woven in Iran, Afghanistan, and Turkmenistan; Turkoman-design rugs are woven in Pakistan and India.

MEMLING GUL The Memling Gul is a stepped-hook polygon motif named after the 15th-century Flemish artist Hans Memling, who used rugs with this motif in many of his paintings. This small motif may appear repeated in multiple rows in the field or encased within an octagon and repeated in rows throughout the field. These guls are used in Caucasian, Turkish, and northwest Persian rugs.

BORDERS
◆

The border of an Oriental rug is made up of a series of bands or stripes which frame the field and focal point of the rug. The standard arrangement is from three to seven borders, with a wide main border flanked by minor borders and guard stripes. Some Chinese rugs have no borders and occasionally have designs that appear to continue off the edge of the carpet.

Border motifs vary to complement the design used in the field of the rug. Like the field design, they are rectilinear or

REPEATED MOTIF

**FLOWER AND
MEANDERING VINE**

curvilinear. Border designs can be divided into groups by the type of motif used: repeated motif, flower and vine, serrated leaf and wineglass, cartouche, Kufic, Shekeri, and Herati. In addition to these designs, numerous variations are used.

Repeated motifs such as flower heads, rosettes, tulips, carnations, lotus, and peonies are repeated in the main border. In addition, repeated stars, octagons, and other geometric motifs are used as minor border designs.

A flower and meandering vine border consists of a flower head with leaves connected by a continuous vine. This type of design is used in Persian, Turkish, and some Turkoman rugs.

A serrated leaf and wineglass border is used primarily in Caucasian rugs and is also found in Balouchi rugs. It consists of a wineglass motif flanked by serrated leaves.

Cartouche motifs are used most frequently in Persian and Turkish rugs. The cartouches may be filled with a flower and leaf pattern, poetic inscriptions, or proverbs in Persian or Arabic.

Kufic border designs are based on rectilinear Arabic script. This type of border design is used most often in Caucasian rugs.

The Shekeri design is composed of a meandering vine with boteh. This type of design is often found in the rugs of Ingeles and Seraband as well as in other rugs from the Hamadan area.

The Herati border design is not the same as the Herati design used in the field of a rug. The Herati border pattern is most frequently used in Persian border designs, and consists

**SERRATED LEAF AND
WINEGLASS**

CARTOUCHE

KUFIC

SHEKERI

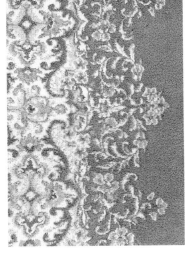

AUBUSSON

RECIPROCAL

RUNNING DOG

INSCRIPTIONS

HERATI

of a series of palmettes or lotus flowers connected by meandering vine leaves.

An Aubusson border arrangement has no linear form. It is curvilinear, formed by floral sprays, swirls, vines, and leafs. This type of border is frequently used in Kerman and Aubusson-design rugs woven in India.

Minor borders also are rectilinear or curvilinear, and can be classified by their type of design: reciprocating, flower and meandering vine, repeating motif, running dog, or diagonal stripes.

Carpets occasionally are woven with an inscription or signature. Inscriptions are obvious when woven in the background or in a cartouche; others are not as apparent and blend with a design or a border pattern. Inscriptions most often encountered are in Persian or Armenian script, although inscriptions also are made in Hebrew, Sanskrit, or Arabic as well as Western, Cyrillic, and other alphabets. Persian inscriptions are read from right to left, although numbers are read left to right, as in the West. Armenian inscriptions are read from left to right. The inscription may be a poem, proverb, prayer, dedication to a church or mosque, or simply the signature or the initials of the weaver.

Ա ա Բ բ Գ գ Դ դ Ե ե Զ զ Է է Ը ը Թ թ Ժ ժ Ի ի Լ լ Խ խ Ծ ծ

A a P p G g D d E e Z z E e E e T t Zh zh I i L l Kh kh Tz tz

Կ կ Հ հ Ձ ձ Ղ ղ Ճ ճ Մ մ Յ յ Ն ն Շ շ Ո ո Չ չ Պ պ Ջ ջ Ռ ռ

K k H h Dz dz Gh gh Ch ch M m Y y N n Sh sh O o Ch ch B b Dj dj R r

Ս ս Վ վ Տ տ Ր ր Ց ց Ու ու Փ փ Ք ք Օ o Ֆ ֆ

S s V v T t R r Ts ts V v P p K k O o F f

THE ARMENIAN ALPHABET

ح ح	چ چ	ج ج	ث ث	ت ت	پ پ	ب ب	ا، الف، آ
H	CH	J	S	T	P	B	A

ش ش	س س	ژ ز	ز ز	ر ر	ذ ذ	د د	خ خ
SH	S	ZH	Z	R	Z	D	KH

ق ق	ف ف	غ غ	ع ع	ظ ظ	ط ط	ض ض	ص ص
G	F	G	A	Z	T	Z	S

ی ی	ه ه ه	و و	ن ن	م م	ل ل	گ گ	ک ک
I, Y	H	V	N	M	L	G	K

THE PERSIAN ALPHABET

١	٢	٣	٤	٥	٦	٧	٨	٩	١٠
1	2	3	4	5	6	7	8	9	10

PERSIAN NUMBERS

DATES
◆

Both Islamic and Christian dates can be found in Oriental rugs. Islamic dates, such as those found on Persian and Caucasian rugs, are written in Arabic numbers and can be easily converted into their Western equivalent.

PERSIAN INSCRIPTION
"AMAL BROTHERS"

ARMENIAN INSCRIPTION
AND DATE "ASAK
MANASIAN, 1905"

With a few exceptions, Islamic dates are based on the Muslim calendar, which begins with the Hegira, the Prophet Muhammad's flight from Mecca on July 16, A.D. 622. The Muslim calendar is based on the lunar year and is shorter than the solar-based Gregorian calendar used in Europe and the Western Hemisphere. The Muslim calendar is typically the basis for dates in Arabic numbers found in antique and semiantique rugs. The figure at left shows a simple mathematical procedure for converting these dates. An alternative is to just add 585 to the year; this will be accurate to within five years of the actual date and is close enough for a quick estimate.

Dates written in Western numerals can be found in rugs woven in the Caucasus, Iran, and Turkey. The majority of these rugs are woven by Armenian weavers and their dates are based on the Gregorian calendar and can be interpreted as they were written. Occasionally Arabic numbers are used for a date based on the Gregorian system.

In some Armenian rugs the dates are written in the form of a fraction. The number representing the month is placed over the number representing the day of the month, and the year is split into two sets of two numbers on either side of the fraction. For example, $19 \frac{8}{15} 39$ would be August 15, 1939. Armenian dates are frequently followed by a composite letter Առ, which means "in the year of."

١٣١٦

To convert to Western numerals (1316)
Divide the Islamic date by 33 (1316 ÷ 33 = 40)
Subtract the quotient from the year (1316 − 40 = 1276)
Add 622 (1276 + 622 = 1898)

CONVERSION OF ISLAMIC DATES

TABRIZ, 6'6" X 9'9"

five

*I*ran is mainly a plateau bordered by the Alburz Mountains on the north and the Zagros Mountains on the south and west. The Dasht-e-Lut and Dasht-e-Kavir deserts occupy much of east-central Iran. For hundreds of years Iran was basically an agricultural country until the discovery of vast oil deposits in the early 1900s provided a basis of economic development.

The majority of the Iranians are of Aryan origin. The remaining population is composed of Armenians, Azerbaijanis, Balouchis, Kurds, Arabs, Bakhtiaris, Turkomans, Qashqa'is, Afshars, and Lurs. The majority of Iranians are Muslims of the Shiite sect. The Armenian minority are Christians. These ethnic groups weave rugs that reflect the origins of the weavers and their environs.

TURKEY
MESHKINSHAHR
Caspian Sea
TURKMENISTAN
TABRIZ
ARDEBIL
MERIGEH
QUCHAN
MASHAD
BIJAR
SANANDAJ
TEHRAN
VERAMIN
TORBAT-E-
HEYDARYEH
HAMADAN
QUM
ARAK
KASHAN
TABAS
NAIN
BIRJAND
SHAHR-E-KORD
ISFAHAN
MUD
YEZD
AFGHANISTAN
IRAQ
ABADEH
KERMAN
KUWAIT
SHIRAZ
Persian Gulf
SAUDI
ARABIA
PAKISTAN
Gulf of Oman

MAJOR RUG-WEAVING
CENTERS OF IRAN

Iranian rugs are named either for the town or village where they were woven or for the tribal group that wove them. Rugs from small villages are often named after the larger town where they are sold. A wide variety of designs and color combinations are used, and the style and colors vary between towns and tribal groups.

City rugs are woven with cotton or silk warp and weft threads, and tend to have floral and curvilinear patterns. The weaving is done in small ateliers with several looms or in larger workshops with many looms. Two or more weavers work side by side, on vertical looms, depending on the size of the carpet to be produced. In some areas, such as Tabriz, weaving in workshops is done by men; in other areas, such as Isfahan, women do the weaving.

Individuals also weave in their homes. A vertical loom may be set up in the corner of a room and a mother and daughters may work together or separately on a carpet. In some households weaving is a family project, the husband and wife as well as the older children contributing to the work. In towns, women purchase the wool to be used; this wool has already been spun and dyed. They also buy cartoons of the pattern to be followed. The weaver is free to interpret the design at will or directly follow the cartoon and the colors dictated.

Rugs woven by tribal and nomadic weavers have wool warps and wefts and are woven by women on horizontal looms. Many of the geometric patterns produced are learned in childhood; some women are so skilled that they create their own design as they weave. Nomadic women do most of their own spinning, dyeing, and weaving. The wool they use comes from their own sheep and is supplemented, when needed, with purchased wool.

Many of the tribes are seminomadic, migrating only between their winter and summer homes. In the summer nomadic women can be seen sitting on their looms under tents, weaving their carpets. Some nomads live in tents; others live in dried-earth houses once they reach their destination.

Inscriptions and dates are occasionally found in Persian rugs. The majority of the inscriptions are in the Persian script and the dates are written in Arabic numbers. Most of the ethnic minorities also use the Persian script for their inscriptions. A few Persian rugs have inscriptions in Armenian script and Western dates.

AZERBAIJAN

Azerbaijan was divided by the Treaty of Turkmanchai in 1828; control of the area south of the Araks River was given to Persia; of the north, to Russia. The Iranian provinces of West Azerbaijan and East Azerbaijan are between Turkey and Iraq on the west and the Caspian Sea on the east; to the north is Azerbaijan. Tabriz is the capital and the largest city of East Azerbaijan; Urmiyeh is the capital of West Azerbaijan. Azeri Turks make up the largest portion of the population in the Azerbaijan provinces; however, Kurds, Armenians, and Shahsavans also inhabit the area.

TABRIZ The city of Tabriz is located in northwest Iran, at the foothills of Mount Sahand, near the Turkish, Azerbaijani, and Armenian borders. For centuries Tabriz has been a commercial center because of its location at the juncture of major trade routes to the Far East and southern Persia.

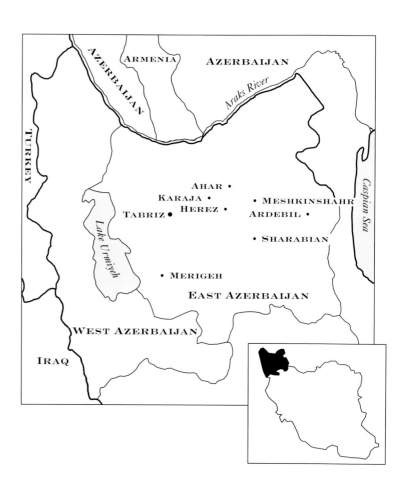

EAST AND WEST
AZERBAIJAN PROVINCES

TABRIZ

◆

KNOT
symmetrical

WARP
cotton, occasionally silk

WEFT
two shoots; cotton,
occasionally silk

PILE
coarse, heavy wool in
medium quality; soft wool
with silk used as highlights
in finer qualities

ENDS
knotted fringe at both ends

SIDES
single cord, overcast
with wool

◆

Tabriz carpets are woven in Tabriz and numerous small surrounding villages. The weavers here are among the fastest and most skilled in Iran. They use a tool that enables the weaver to tie a knot a second. Called the *Tabriz hook*, it consists of a knife, similar to that used in other weaving centers, with a small hook at its tip. This implement enables the weaver to isolate a pair of warp threads, loop a strand of wool around the warps, then cut the strand free, all in one continuous motion.

Weaving in the Tabriz area can vary greatly in quality, ranging from some of the world's finest carpets to a poor, "bazaar" quality. Common qualities of Tabriz rugs range from 30 to 90 knots per line or *radj*. A *radj* is a measure which equals the length of a Persian cigarette, approximately 3 inches (7 centimeters).

In fine-quality Tabriz rugs, a thin white cotton cord is used for the warp and weft threads. The wool used for the pile is an excellent quality and trimmed short. Small amounts of silk are often used to accentuate certain designs and motifs. In rugs of medium to coarse quality, a thick cotton warp is used and a heavy wool of medium length is used for the pile.

During the last half of the 19th century, pure silk rugs were woven in Tabriz, with designs reminiscent of Turkish prayer rugs. Today, silk rugs are woven in Prayer designs as well as the Medallion and Shah Abbas designs. Some silk rugs have a gold metallic thread, woven in a soumak stitch (see Chapter 14), which is used to accentuate certain motifs. Tabriz silk rugs are finely woven and are of excellent quality; this is reflected in their high prices. Silk rugs make up only a small percentage of the rugs woven in the Tabriz district.

During the 1980s some Tabriz rugs were woven with polyester warp and weft threads—though polyester has proven to be unsatisfactory because of its elasticity. Rugs woven with polyester warp and weft threads do not lie completely flat, and even after blocking, the bumps will reoccur.

The *Taba Tabae* Tabriz, popular on the North American markets in the 1970s, is a good-quality rug and reasonably priced. The Taba Tabae is woven on a foundation of thick cotton warp and weft threads. The pile is a heavy, thick wool from the Maku area, medium length. The most common designs employed are the Hunting, Garden, Medallion, and Herati designs. The Taba Tabaes are woven in earth tones of brown, gold, green, ivory, blue, and pastel colors.

In Tabriz rugs, a wide variety of designs are woven in both curvilinear and rectilinear formats: the Zil-i-Sultan, Medallion, Shah Abbas, Picture, and Mahi (also known as Herati). One of the new designs, "Mahi Tabriz," is composed of small Herati motifs repeated throughout the field of the carpet. This repetition is carried through the medallion, spandrels, as well as the field, with contrasting background colors between the design areas of the carpet, for example, the medallion and field. This color change gives an overall impression of a medallion and spandrel carpet rather than one of a repeated, regimented format.

The wide variety of color combinations used in Tabriz rugs is very appealing to both the European and North American markets. Background colors range from deep, rich tones of blue

BACK OF TABRIZ

and red to pastel shades, taupe, and ivory. Black-background rugs are also woven.

Tabriz rugs are among the most popular Persian rugs. Fine-quality Tabrizes are tightly woven and very durable. Prices vary according to quality, and they are available in almost any size from small mats and runners to the large gallery size. In addition, a large number of round rugs and square rugs in sizes up to 13 feet (4 meters) are available.

HEREZ The Herez weaving district lies about 40 miles (65 kilometers) east of Tabriz and is composed of about thirty weaving villages. The rugs woven in these villages are similar in structure and design; the major difference is the quality. The names of some of these villages are used in the Oriental rug trade to denote the quality, although there is no correlation with where the rug was actually woven. The quality grades of Herez-area rugs in descending order are Herez, Meriban, and Gorevan.

The classic Herez design is composed of a large-scale geometric medallion and corner spandrels with stylized leaf and palmettes in the field. The main border contains the Herati border pattern. Another pattern woven in the Herez area is that of repeated palmettes and stylized leaves.

Late-19th-century Herez rugs have soft, muted tones of pink, khaki, ivory, rust, and light and dark blue. New Herez

HEREZ

◆

KNOT
symmetrical

WARP
cotton, thick

WEFT
two shoots,
light-blue cotton

PILE
medium; heavy,
good-quality wool

ENDS
plain or knotted fringe
at both ends

SIDES
two-cord cotton selvedge,
or overcast with wool

◆

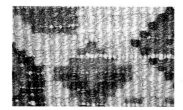

BACK OF HEREZ

HEREZ, 6' X 9'

rugs have bright shades of red, blue, green, brown, and white.

The quality of rugs woven in the Herez district varies greatly. The better Herez rugs are woven with a good quality of wool and will withstand wear quite well.

Sharabian rugs are woven in villages south of the Herez area. These rugs are coarsely knotted on thick cotton warp threads. They are very thick bodied, due to the severe depression of their warp threads. Sharabians are brightly colored with red, blue, yellow, and green.

The majority of Herez rugs are woven in large sizes, 6 feet 6 inches by 9 feet 9 inches (2 by 3 meters) and larger.

Serapi. The name "Serapi" has become associated with fine old Herez rugs. Although no village or town by this name exists in Iran, the name has become synonymous with these Herez-area carpets. Serapi carpets are characterized by a large-scale central medallion and spandrels with a field sparsely filled with geometric leaf motifs. The colors are soft and muted with shades of brick red, white, and light blue. Old rugs often are found worn to the base of the knots. Most rugs were woven in large sizes, 7 by 10 feet (213 by 305 centimeters) and larger.

KARAJA (GARADJEH) Karaja rugs are woven in Karaja and in the small surrounding villages in the foothills of the Karadagh range, approximately 35 miles (55 kilometers) northeast of Tabriz. These rugs are easily identified by their distinctive geometric medallions. Three small medallions alternate between a latch-hook motif and a rectilinear emblem-type motif. The same small motifs are used in large-size rugs but are sequenced in rows to fill the field. More recently, room-size rugs have been woven with a rectilinear medallion design similar to that of Herez. The background color is usually madder red, with navy blue used for the main border. Occasionally these colors are reversed.

The wool used for the pile is an excellent-quality local wool. Older Karaja rugs are more finely woven than their modern counterparts and their designs are more intricate. After World War II, Karaja rugs were very coarsely woven with a long, shaggy wool, which yielded designs that were blurred in appearance. These coarsely woven rugs did not withstand wear very well.

KARAJA

◆

KNOT
symmetrical

WARP
thick cotton

WEFT
single shoot, thick cotton

PILE
medium long;
good-quality wool

ENDS
knotted fringe at both ends

SIDES
two cords, wrapped with
cotton selvedge or overcast
with wool

◆

BACK OF KARAJA

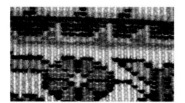

BACK OF ARDEBIL

KARAJA, 3' x 4'

ARDEBIL

◆

KNOT
symmetrical

WARP
cotton (wool in older rugs)

WEFT
two shoots, cotton (wool in
older rugs)

PILE
short, good-quality wool, or a
combination of wool and silk

ENDS
knotted fringe at both ends

SIDES
single cord, wrapped with
wefts or overcast
with wool

◆

Since the 1960s, however, the quality of Karajas has greatly improved.

The majority of Karaja rugs were woven in small sizes and runners. Used Karaja rugs are widely available. Both new and old Karaja rugs are reasonably priced and are a good value.

ARDEBIL Ardebil is an ancient city, situated 20 miles (32 kilometers) south of the border with Azerbaijan and 27 miles (45 kilometers) west of the Caspian Sea.

Designs woven in Ardebil rugs resemble those woven in the Caucasian weaving districts of Shirvan and Kuba. One of the most common designs used is that of three-notched, diamond-shaped medallions on a field with small stars, polygons, rosettes, birds, and animals. The ram's horn motif, associated with the town of Perepedil in the Kuba district, is also frequently woven.

Ardebil rugs are more finely woven than those of the neighboring town of Meshkinshar. The designs woven in Ardebil are more intricate and the pile is clipped shorter. In some Ardebil rugs, the pile of an entire medallion or design

ARDEBIL, 6' X 9'

MERIGEH, 3' X 5'

MERIGEH

◆

KNOT
asymmetrical

WARP
silk

WEFT
cotton

PILE
silk

ENDS
small kelim with knotted
fringe at both ends

SIDES
single cord, overcast
with silk

◆

is woven in silk, with the remaining pile woven with wool. The lustrous silk accentuates and highlights the entire motif. Woven in a variety of color combinations and sizes, Ardebil rugs range from small mats to room-size rugs and runners.

MERIGEH (MERAGHEH) The town of Merigeh is located about 42 miles (70 kilometers) south of Tabriz. The weavers here specialize in the production of inexpensive silk rugs. These rugs resemble Qum silk rugs in design and are often sold as Qum silks. Merigeh silk rugs are not as finely woven and have a stiffer body than silk rugs woven in Qum.

The medallion design with spandrels is most frequently woven. A central medallion is superimposed on a field of detached floral sprays. The common color combinations are of ivory, red, turquoise, and blue. The majority of Merigeh rugs are woven in small sizes, 3 feet 3 inches by 5 feet (100 by 152 centimeters).

MESHKIN Meshkin carpets are woven in and around the small town of Meshkinshar, about 50 miles (80 kilometers) northwest of Ardebil on the northern road to Tabriz.

The designs used in Meshkin rugs show a strong Caucasian influence. The large octagonal medallions resemble those woven in the rugs of Kazak. The color palette is limited: blue, brown, gold, and rust for the motifs, with beige used for the background.

The majority of Meshkin carpets are loosely woven. They come in large sizes, 6 feet 6 inches by 9 feet 9 inches (2 by 3 meters) and larger; however, small sizes are also made.

KURDISTAN

Kurdistan is a vast politically undefined area encompassing northeast Iraq, northwest Iran, northeast Syria, and eastern Turkey. The Kurdistan province of Iran is a mountainous area representing only a small portion of land inhabited by Kurds.

The majority of the inhabitants of the Kurdistan province are Kurds, who reside in villages and small towns. The Kurds are one of the largest and most important of the tribal groups in Iran. Traditionally they lived a nomadic and seminomadic

MESHKIN

◆

KNOT
symmetrical

WARP
wool or thick cotton

WEFT
two shoots, wool or cotton

PILE
wool, medium in length

ENDS
knotted fringe at both ends

SIDES
single cord, overcast
with wool

◆

KURDISTAN PROVINCE

KNOT
symmetrical

WARP
wool or cotton

WEFT
one or two shoots;
wool or cotton

PILE
wool, medium long

ENDS
kelim at one end with
knotted fringe at the other, or
knotted fringe at both ends

SIDES
one or two cords,
overcast with wool or
goat's hair

◆

existence. In Kurdistan three distinctive types of Kurdish weaving are done: Senna, Bijar, and the Kurdish village rugs.

KURDISH RUGS The majority of Kurdish rugs from the Persian Kurdistan area are woven by Senjabi, Jaff, Gurani, and Kolyhai Kurds. Characteristics of Kurdish tribal rugs vary according to the location of the weaving group and the individual weaving the rug. With few exceptions, individual rugs are hard to attribute to a specific Kurdish group because structural characteristics are so variable. Kurdish rugs are woven with wool and cotton used for the warp and weft threads. In general the Kurds are prolific weavers, making small rugs as well as storage bags, saddlebags, and salt bags.

A wide variety of designs were woven by Kurdish weavers. They used the Gul-i-Henna, Herati, Boteh, Medallion, and repeated geometric patterns. The Kurds frequently used a central medallion with anchorlike motifs.

The Jaff Kurds, who reside in both Iran and Iraq, have a unique way of knotting their rugs. Rows of knots are staggered, so a knot is tied on the same pair of warp threads only every second row of knots. This type of weave allows a more curvilinear outline to the motifs. Jaff Kurds also are known for

KURDISH, 3' X 5'6"

KOLYAI

◆

KNOT
asymmetrical

WARP
cotton

WEFT
single, cotton

PILE
wool, medium

ENDS
knotted fringe at both ends

SIDES
single cord, overcast
with wool

◆

weaving a colorful design composed of diamond-shaped compartments. Within each of the compartments is a latch-hooked motif. This pattern is used on numerous small bags and rugs.

KOLYAI (KOLYAHI, QULYAHI) Kolyai rugs are woven by the Kolyai group of Kurds who reside in an area between Qorveh and Songor. Rugs woven by the Kolyai are similar to the rugs of Hamadan in structure. The design used for the background is unique: a hexagonal field is composed of a tone-on-tone motif, camel on ivory, within a brown lattice framework. A central medallion is often used in combination with this field pattern. Older rugs were woven primarily in small sizes. Currently sizes up to 7 by 10 feet (215 by 305 centimeters) are woven.

SENNA (SANANDAJ) Senna rugs are woven in the town of Sanandaj, the capital and major city in the Province of Kurdistan. Sanandaj is approximately 90 miles (150 kilometers) northwest of Hamadan. The population is primarily Kurdish.

KOLYAI, 7' X 10'

SENNA, 3'5" X 5'

SENNA

◆

KNOT
symmetrical

WARP
cotton or silk

WEFT
one shoot, cotton or silk

PILE
wool, cut short

ENDS
small kelim, plain or knotted
at both ends

SIDES
single cord, overcast
with wool or
occasionally silk

◆

The weaving in Sanandaj is quite different from other types of Kurdish weaving. Cotton is used for the warp and weft threads and a single cotton weft is passed between each row of knots. Senna carpets are finely woven. The body of a Senna is relatively thin when compared, say, to a Bijar.

At the turn of the century, a group of Senna rugs were woven with multicolored warp threads. These rugs were woven with seven different color bands (*haft rang*) of silk warp threads. The sides of the *haft rang* Sennas are usually overcast with purple silk. Rugs of this type are very finely woven.

The design most commonly found in Senna rugs is a central, lozenge-shaped medallion on a dark-blue field, with small repeated Herati motifs. Other designs woven include offset repeated boteh on an ivory background and bouquets of flowers repeated throughout the field.

The colors used in new Senna rugs are bright: red, white, and blue are primary, with accents of yellow and green. In older rugs the color palette is much more muted, with tones of light blue, yellow, rose red, dark blue, yellow, and beige.

Most Senna rugs are small, 3 feet 6 inches by 5 feet (105 by 150 centimeters) to 4 feet 6 inches by 7 feet (135 by 210 centimeters); however, large rugs are also woven. Senna is also known for the fine quality of its kelims (see Chapter 14).

BIJAR The small town of Bijar is located about 40 miles (65 kilometers) northeast of Sanandaj and 90 miles (150 kilometers) northwest of Hamadan. The rugs are woven in Bijar and numerous surrounding villages. Some of the finest Bijar rugs are woven by Kurdish weavers in the village of Halvai. Other finely woven Bijar rugs are woven in and around the town of Tekab by Afshars who have settled there.

At the end of the 19th century a distinctive group of carpets, known as Garrus (see page 10), were woven in what is now the district of Bijar. Most Garrus rugs have wool warps and three shoots of red wool weft threads. These carpets are characterized by a design composed of leaf palmettes, shield medallions, and straplike red arabesques, on a dark-blue background.*

BACK OF SENNA

*Annette Ittig, "A Group of Inscribed Carpets from Persian Kurdistan," *Hali* IV: 2 (1981), 124–27.

KNOT
symmetrical

WARP
cotton (wool in older rugs)

WEFT
two or three shoots, cotton,
wool, or both; dyed
red or blue

PILE
wool, cut short

ENDS
kelim at one end, with
knotted fringe at the other

SIDES
single cord, overcast
with wool

◆

A combination of the Herati and Medallion designs is the most frequently used pattern in Bijar rugs; a lozenge-shaped medallion is superimposed on a field filled with the repeated Herati motif. On occasion the central medallion and spandrels are filled with the Herati motif on a plain navy or camel-colored field. Another design frequently used consists of a central medallion on a field filled with roses, vines, and leaves. The roses are repeated in the main border.

Wagirehs are also woven in Bijar. A Wagireh is a sampler, a composite of the various field and border designs woven in the area and incorporated into one rug. Wagirehs are woven in small sizes.

One of the structural features characteristic of Bijar carpets is the thickness of the body of the rug. Two or three weft threads are used, one thick and either one or two thin. These wefts are very tightly packed together, which causes a severe depression of the warp threads. As a result, Bijars have a very dense and tight weave and wear extremely well.

Bijar rugs are woven in a variety of sizes from small mats to large gallery sizes. Runners of varying lengths are also woven.

BIJAR, 3'3" X 7'

The Hamadan weaving district is composed of hundreds of small villages and towns within a fifty-mile radius of the city of Hamadan. The city of Hamadan serves as a collection center for the rugs woven in the area. Rugs of Dergazine, Ingeles, Bibikabad, Hoseinabad, and numerous other small villages are sold in the markets in Hamadan.

HAMADAN The city of Hamadan is located 204 miles (340 kilometers) southwest of Tehran, at the foot of Mount Alvand. It is one of the oldest permanently settled towns in the world, being inhabited for over several thousand years. Originally known as Ecbatana, it was the capital of the Median kingdom in the 6th century B.C. The tombs of Esther and Mordecai are located in Hamadan.

The weave of Hamadan rugs is characterized by a combination of one shoot of weft and warps on the same level. This combination yields a flat appearance to the back of the rug.

Both rectilinear and curvilinear designs are woven in rugs of the Hamadan area. Rectilinear rod medallions, boteh, and

HAMADAN

◆

KNOT
symmetrical

WARP
cotton, on the same level

WEFT
one shoot; cotton or wool in some older rugs

PILE
medium,
excellent-quality wool

ENDS
kelim at one end, with plain fringe at the other

SIDES
single cord, overcast with wool

◆

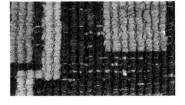

BACK OF BIJAR

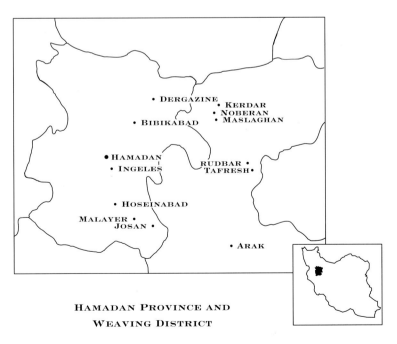

HAMADAN PROVINCE AND
WEAVING DISTRICT

BACK OF HAMADAN

HAMADAN, 3' X 6'

MASLAGHAN, 4'6" X 6'6"

MASLAGHAN

◆

KNOT
symmetrical

WARP
cotton

WEFT
one shoot, cotton

PILE
lustrous,
excellent-quality wool

ENDS
kelim at one end, with
knotted fringe at the other

SIDES
single cord, overcast
with wool

◆

Herati patterns are frequently used. The weave in Hamadan rugs varies from coarse to medium; older Hamadans have a thinner pile and a much tighter weave than rugs currently woven. Excellent-quality wool is used for the pile which yields rugs that wear exceptionally well.

The largest majority of Hamadan rugs are woven in small sizes, from mats to rugs approximately 4 by 7 feet. Room-size rugs and runners are also made. A large number of used Hamadan rugs are available and are quite often in good condition. They are usually much less expensive than other rugs of similar age.

MASLAGHAN Rugs known as Maslaghan are woven in the villages of Nobaran, Kerdar, and Maslaghan in the Saveh district southwest of Tehran. These villages are known for weaving a unique design in which a lightning-bolt motif separates the field from the corner spandrels. The background color is usually red with the central medallion and the spandrels dark blue. The spandrels are filled with small multicolored flower head motifs.

The wool used for the pile is a lustrous, excellent-quality wool which is trimmed relatively short. Older Maslaghans are more finely woven than their modern counterparts. Both new and

TAFRESH, 2'6" x 6'9"

TAFRESH

◆

KNOT
symmetrical or asymmetrical

WARP
cotton

WEFT
one shoot, cotton

PILE
wool

ENDS
knotted fringe at both ends

SIDES
single cord, overcast
with wool

◆

RUDBAR

◆

KNOT
symmetrical

WARP
cotton

WEFT
single, cotton

PILE
wool

ENDS
knotted fringe at both ends

SIDES
single cord, overcast
with wool

◆

old Maslaghans are quite durable, reasonably priced, and a good value. Maslaghan rugs usually are woven in 3 by 5 foot (90 by 150 centimeter) and 4 by 6 foot (120 by 180 centimeter) sizes.

TAFRESH The town of Tafresh is located 50 miles (80 kilometers) west of Qum. Rugs are woven in Tafresh and the surrounding area.

The designs used in Tafresh are floral. A lobed medallion with detached floral sprays or a vase of flowers with floral sprays and birds are designs commonly used. In the runner format, medallions sequenced to fill the field are interspersed with floral sprays. In small runners a medallion is often flanked by a pair of vases with flowers. The background is either ivory or various shades of red.

The majority of Tafresh rugs are woven in small sizes and in runners of various lengths. These rugs are woven with excellent-quality wool and withstand wear very well. They are recommended for use on stairs and in halls.

RUDBAR (ROUDBAR) The village of Rudbar is located just northwest of Tafresh. It is known for its production of small carpets and runners. The runners are woven in varying lengths. The Herati design is commonly used on an ivory background.

These are excellent-quality rugs, good for use on stairs and in halls. They will withstand wear very well.

DERGAZINE (DERGEZINE, DARGAZIN) The Dergazine weaving district consists of sixty small villages, 50 miles (80 kilometers) northeast of Hamadan. Carpet weaving

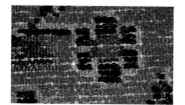

BACK OF DERGAZINE

DERGAZINE, 4' x 6'

INGELES, 4' x 6'

DERGAZINE

◆

KNOT
symmetrical

WARP
cotton

WEFT
one shoot, cotton

PILE
wool, medium in length

ENDS
kelim at one end, knotted
fringe at the other

SIDES
single cord, overcast
with wool

◆

has been done in this area since the 17th century.

During the 1920s and '30s Dergazine rugs were very popular in North America. They were woven with a central medallion, spandrels, and a field of detached floral sprays. Red and dark blue were the most common colors used for the field. These Dergazine rugs resembled Sarouk carpets in design but were not as expensive. During this period the majority of Dergazines were washed and painted, like the Sarouks.

Currently Dergazine rugs are not as finely woven as their earlier counterparts, nor are their designs as crisp and clear. The Medallion design with detached floral sprays is still used, with either a red or dark-blue background.

Dergazine rugs are woven in a variety of sizes from small mats to room-size rugs and runners. They are of excellent-quality wool and are very durable.

INGELES (INGELAS, INJILAS, ANGELAS) Ingeles is a small town south of Hamadan. Rugs woven in Ingeles and the surrounding area are among the finest of the Hamadan-area rugs. Like others from the area, they are woven with a single weft between the rows of knots and the warps on the same level. This type of weave gives a flat appearance to the back of the rug.

The design most frequently used in Ingeles rugs is the

INGELES

♦

KNOT
symmetrical

WARP
cotton

WEFT
single shoot, cotton

PILE
wool, medium in length

ENDS
kelim at one end, with plain
fringe at the other

SIDES
one cord, overcast
with wool

♦

Herati pattern. It may be repeated in rows throughout the field or used in combination with a central medallion and spandrels. Occasionally the Herati pattern is used with spandrels only. A repeated Boteh pattern is also used, but less frequently. The common colors are cherry red, ivory, light blue, and dark blue.

The border arrangement most often associated with Ingeles rugs is that of a Shekeri design main border on a white background, flanked by dark-blue minor borders.

The majority of rugs woven in Ingeles are in small sizes to 4 feet 6 inches by 7 feet (135 by 215 centimeters) or runners.

MALAYER The small town of Malayer lies halfway between Hamadan and Arak. Weaving is done in Malayer and over two hundred area villages.

The villages northwest of Malayer, toward Hamadan, weave a carpet very similar to the Hamadan in structure. These rugs are woven with a symmetrical knot and a single shoot of weft between the rows of knots. The designs frequently used are the Boteh, Herati, and Medallion-and-Corner.

The villages to the southeast of Malayer, toward Arak, weave a more finely knotted carpet, very similar in weave to Sarouk. These rugs are sometimes referred to as "Malayer Sarouks." They are asymmetrically knotted with two shoots of weft passing between the rows of knots. The Medallion-and-Corner design is commonly used. Josan is the most important of the villages of this area.

MALAYER, 5' X 13'

KNOT

symmetrical or asymmetrical

WARP

cotton

WEFT

one or two shoots, cotton

PILE

wool, medium long

ENDS

kelim at one end, with
knotted fringe at the other

SIDES

one cord, overcast
with wool

ARAK

KNOT

asymmetrical

WARP

cotton

WEFT

two shoots, dyed blue cotton

PILE

wool, medium to
medium long

ENDS

kelim at one end, with
knotted fringe at the other

SIDES

single cord, overcast
with wool

MARKAZI PROVINCE AND ARAK WEAVING AREA

The Arak weaving area lies to the east of the Hamadan area and is composed of the towns of Arak, Sarouk, Seraband, Ferahan, and Lillihan. With the exception of Lillihan, all of these towns use the asymmetrical knot with two shoots of wefts.

ARAK (SULTANABAD) Arak, formally known as Sultanabad, is located 90 miles (144 kilometers) southeast of Hamadan and 194 miles (297 kilometers) southwest of Tehran. Arak has been a commercial center since the 19th century and has served as the major market center for carpets woven in Mushkabad, Sarouk, and Lillihan, as well as the Kemereh, Feraghan, and Saraband districts.

Rugs from the Arak-area villages share common structural characteristics but vary in the fineness of weave. The names of some Arak-area villages and towns are used to denote the quality of the rug, although it is not necessarily where the rug was woven. For example, rugs labeled as "Arak" and "Mahal"

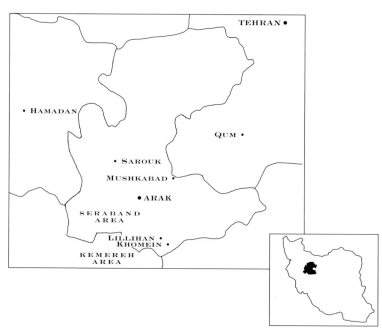

MARKAZI PROVINCE AND ARAK WEAVING AREA

MAHAL, 4' X 6'

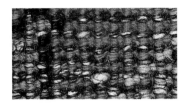

BACK OF MAHAL

denote quality, rather than the village where the rug was woven. The quality grades of Arak-area rugs in descending order are Sarouk, Arak, Sultanabad, Mahal, and Mushkabad.

Herati, Shah Abbas, and central medallion patterns are frequently woven in the Arak area. A large floral medallion on a red open field surrounded by Aubusson-type floral border was commonly woven in the Mahal quality. Another pattern frequently used was that of a central medallion combined with a repeated Herati motif filling the field. The background was dark blue.

A variety of formats and sizes are made in the Arak area. In lower-quality rugs, large sizes are the most common, 8 by 10 feet (245 by 305 centimeters) and larger.

ZIEGLER Ziegler carpets were woven in Sultanabad from the early 1880s to the 1920s by Messrs. Ziegler and Company, a firm based in Manchester, England. The Ziegler company introduced a system of supplying weavers with dyed wool yarn and patterns to weave. The company began by exporting Sultanabad-area rugs and expanded into carpet production. Ziegler rugs were woven with designs made for the European market, including repeating floral patterns, Herati, scroll motifs, and central medallion on an open field. The colors used were red, brown, light and dark blue, pink, green, and white. The quality grades vary from rather coarse to finely woven rugs.

◆

KNOT
asymmetrical

WARP
cotton, depressed

WEFT
two shoots, dyed blue cotton

PILE
short, excellent-quality wool

ENDS
kelim at one end, with
knotted fringe at the other

SIDES
single cord, overcast
with wool

◆

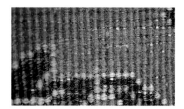

BACK OF SAROUK RUG

SAROUK The town of Sarouk is located about 25 miles (40 kilometers) north of Arak. The name "Sarouk" is also used for denoting the finest-quality rugs woven in the Arak area.

The design most associated with Sarouk rugs is that of detached floral sprays on a rose red background. Rugs of this type became popular in the United States in the 1920s and are still known in the trade as "American Sarouks." The thousands of Sarouks woven for the North American market after World War I had a central floral bouquet with a field containing vases, palmettes, and detached floral sprays. The main border had the Herati border pattern on a dark-blue ground. These Sarouks have a velvety, lustrous pile and they range in size from small mats to gallery size. During the 1920s and '30s the majority of American Sarouks were washed and painted after their arrival in New York.

Late-19th-century Sarouks have more angular patterns than their later counterparts. An oversized blue or cream medallion on a dark blue background was used, the medallion often elegantly outlined. The primary colors are brick red, natural white, and dark blue. Pink and green are used in the motifs.

Currently Sarouk rugs are woven in a variety of designs, both floral and geometric, and in a wide range of color combinations.

SAROUK, 4' x 6'

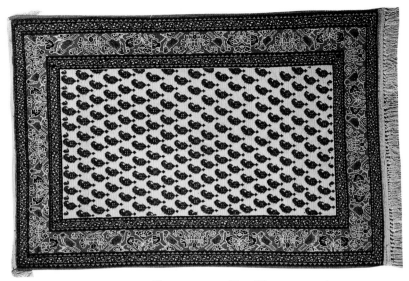

SERABAND, 4' X 6'

SERABAND

◆

KNOT
symmetrical, occasionally
asymmetrical

WARP
cotton

WEFT
two shoots, cotton
(usually dyed blue)

PILE
wool, thick medium-long

ENDS
kelim at one end, with
knotted fringe at the other

SIDES
single cord, overcast
with wool

◆

SERABAND (SARABAND) Seraband rugs are woven in the three hundred or more villages in the Seraband (Sarawan) district, about 62 miles (100 kilometers) southwest of Arak. Carpet weaving has been done in this area for several hundred years.

The classic Seraband design consists of multiple rows of the repeated boteh motif, surrounded by a Shekeri design main border on a white background. The Medallion-and-Corner pattern is occasionally used in combination with a repeated boteh pattern; in some rugs only corner medallions are used. Red is the most common background color, although dark blue and white are also found. The Shekeri border is flanked by a series of minor borders. The majority of rugs are woven in room sizes 8 by 10 feet (245 by 305 centimeters) and larger.

Seraband Sarouk rugs are very similar in design to those of Seraband, except that the type of weave is different. The Seraband Sarouk is structurally a Sarouk, woven with an asymmetrical knot, cotton warps, and dyed blue cotton wefts. They are excellent-quality rugs and are more expensive than Serabands. Seraband Sarouks are woven in a variety of sizes.

FERAGHAN The Feraghan district lies just north of Arak. The Herati pattern on a dark-blue background was most

FERAGHAN

◆

KNOT
asymmetrical

WARP
cotton

WEFT
two shoots, cotton

PILE
short, finely trimmed wool

ENDS
knotted fringe at both ends

SIDES
single cord, overcast
with wool

◆

LILLIHAN

◆

KNOT
asymmetrical

WARP
cotton

WEFT
one shoot, cotton

PILE
wool, medium short

ENDS
kelim at one end, with plain
fringe at the other

SIDES
single cord, overcast
with wool

◆

frequently woven. The Mina Khani and Gul-i-Henna patterns also were used. Feraghans have either a dark-blue or a red background, with green used in the motifs. Older Feraghans were woven in elongated format, 8 by 18 feet, and in small sizes.

LILLIHAN (LILIHAN) The village of Lillihan is 25 miles (40 kilometers) south of Arak. Rugs known as Lillihan were woven by Armenians in Lillihan and neighboring villages in the Kemereh valley, a few miles north of Khomein.

Before World War II the majority of rugs woven in Lillihan were sent to North America, in designs and colors that were the fashion there. These rugs were woven with a central medallion and detached floral sprays filling the field or an overall pattern of floral sprays throughout the field. The designs were very similar to those used in Sarouk. The wool used for the pile is soft and velvety and the colors are beautiful shades of azure blue, dark blue, beige, and light gold for the motifs and borders, and rose for the background. During the 1920s, Lillihans were washed and painted.

Many old and semiantique Lillihan rugs are available. Although 9 by 12 foot rugs were woven, the majority of these rugs are found in small sizes, from small mats to 4 feet 6 inches by 7 feet (150 by 210 centimeters).

Currently the rugs woven in Lillihan and the surrounding area are more similar to the Sarouk in structure and design than

LILLIHAN, 4'5" x 6'

to their earlier counterparts; they are thicker with a longer pile. A central medallion design is commonly used. The primary colors used are red, blue, and turquoise, with white and green for the motifs.

TEHRAN PROVINCE AND NORTH CENTRAL IRAN

Tehran is the capital of and largest city in Iran. It lies in the foothills of the Alborz Mountains, at the base of Mount Damavand. Tehran is the center of the Iranian carpet industry. The Tehran carpet bazaar, a labyrinth of passageways lined with hundreds of carpet shops, is one of the largest in the world. Hundreds of thousands of rugs are brought here each year from all areas of the country to be sold throughout the world.

TEHRAN Although Tehran is the center of the Persian carpet industry, carpet weaving there is on a very small scale. Tehran carpets are finely woven with curvilinear patterns. The Shah Abbas, Tree-of-Life, and Prayer designs are frequently

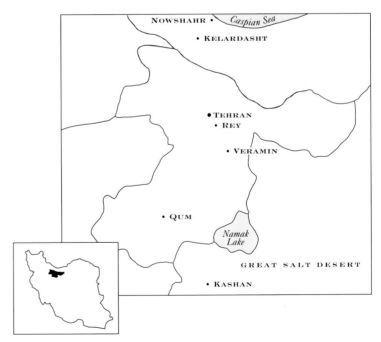

TEHRAN PROVINCE AND NORTH CENTRAL IRAN WEAVING AREAS

TEHRAN

◆

KNOT
asymmetrical

WARP
cotton or silk

WEFT
cotton or silk

PILE
wool or silk

ENDS
small kelim with fringe
at both ends

SIDES
single cord, overcast
with wool

◆

KELARDASHT

◆

KNOT
symmetrical

WARP
wool or cotton

WEFT
two shoots, wool

PILE
wool, medium-long

ENDS
knotted fringe at both ends

SIDES
single cord, overcast
with wool

◆

used. Both wool and silk pile rugs are woven in sizes from 4 by 6 feet (120 by 183 centimeters) to gallery size.

REY Rey, a suburb of Tehran, is the center for carpet washing in Iran. For decades carpets have been taken down to the Cheshmeh Ali stream, scrubbed with soap and water, and laid on the rocky banks to dry in the sun. Currently most rugs are washed in large washing plants in Rey. These plants have large concrete washing floors where dozens of rugs can be washed at the same time. In addition to washing, they also have facilities for shearing the pile, blocking and doing repairs, and for other finishing steps that may be required before the rugs are exported.

KELARDASHT (KALARDASHT) Kelardasht rugs are woven in an area at the base of the Alburz Mountains 25 miles (40 kilometers) south of Nowshahr and the Caspian Sea.

The designs woven in Kelardasht are rectilinear. A large geometric medallion or several medallions are woven on a field with stylized geometric motifs. A stepped white band outlines the medallion or medallions. A red and black common color combination is primarily used.

Kelardasht rugs are tightly woven with a dense pile and are very durable. The majority of rugs are woven in a variety of sizes.

VERAMIN Veramin is a small town approximately 25 miles (40 kilometers) southeast of Tehran in a rich agricultural area. There are two very distinct types of rugs woven in Veramin and the surrounding area: tribal rugs and city rugs. The tribal rugs are woven outside the city of Veramin by Kurds, Lurs, and Shahsavans. These rugs are woven with wool warp and weft threads and in designs that reflect the ethnic origins of the weavers and tribal groups.

Rugs woven in the city of Veramin have a cotton warp and weft threads. The design most commonly woven is the Mina Khani, which consists of repeated flower head motifs surrounded by four similar smaller flowers joined by vines to form a diamond arrangement. The floral motifs are rust red,

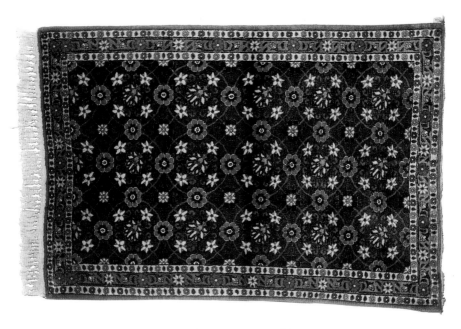

VERAMIN, 3'3" X 5'

VERAMIN

◆

KNOT
asymmetrical

WARP
cotton

WEFT
two shoots, blue cotton

PILE
medium short,
excellent-quality wool

ENDS
small kelim with
knotted fringe

SIDES
single cord, overcast
with wool

◆

yellow, and ivory. The background is blue with red or a lighter shade of blue used for the main border. The Zil-i-Sultan design also is used, with motifs that are relatively large in comparison to the rest of the field. The background of Zil-i-Sultan rugs is usually red or white.

Veramin rugs are finely woven with excellent-quality wool and are quite durable. Many Veramins are given a chemical wash to soften their appearance, even though their unwashed colors are not harsh. They are relatively expensive. Most Veramin rugs come in small sizes, up to 7 by 10 feet (210 by 305 centimeters).

QUM (GHOUM, QOM) The city of Qum is located 90 miles (144 kilometers) south of Tehran at the western edge of the Great Salt Desert (Dasht-e-Kavir). It is one of Iran's holiest cities. Carpet weaving in Qum was begun by weavers from Kashan who set up looms here in the early 1930s.

Both wool and silk rugs are woven in Qum. Wool rugs are finely woven with cotton warp and weft threads. The wool used for the pile is an excellent quality, and kork wool is used in the better-quality Qums. Small amounts of silk often are used in the pile to accentuate certain designs and motifs.

QUM, 4' X 6'

BACK OF QUM

The silk rug production of Qum accounts for more than half of the total number of silk rugs woven in Iran today. Silk pile rugs are woven with silk warps and either cotton or silk for wefts. The silk used is an excellent quality. Because of the expense, silk rugs are usually woven in smaller sizes.

Qum rugs are finely woven with designs that are crisp and well executed. Local weavers use numerous designs and color combinations, many of which have been adopted and adapted from other weaving centers. The most common designs used by the Qum weavers are Central medallion, Prayer, Boteh, Shah Abbas, Panel, and Garden designs.

All sizes, from small mats to room size, are woven in Qum. The combination of designs used and pleasing color combinations make Qum rugs very popular on the market today. Depending on the quality, prices may range from medium to expensive.

QUM

◆

KNOT
asymmetrical

WARP
cotton or silk

WEFT
two shoots, blue, gray,
or beige cotton or silk

PILE
short, excellent-quality
wool, or silk

ENDS
kelim with knotted fringe
at one end and looped
fringe at the other

SIDES
single cord, overcast with
wool or silk

◆

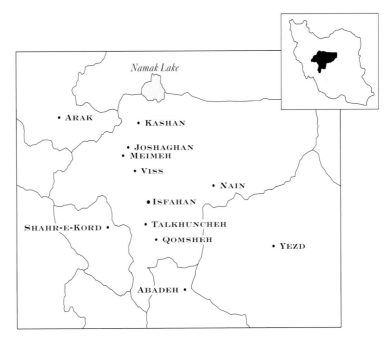

ISFAHAN PROVINCE

ISFAHAN PROVINCE

The province of Isfahan is situated in the center of Iran. Its vast area is bounded by the Great Salt Desert on the east and the foothills of the Zagros Mountains on the west.

The city of Isfahan is the capital and the market center for the province. For centuries Isfahan has been strategically located on ancient as well as modern trade routes.

ISFAHAN Isfahan is regarded as one of the most beautiful cities of the world. Shah Abbas of the Safavid dynasty made it the capital of Persia and moved his court there in 1598. Under his patronage, carpet weaving in Isfahan flourished. During the Afghan invasion in 1722 the industry was severely damaged and it was not until the beginning of the 20th century that it was firmly reestablished.

Early 20th-century Isfahan rugs are not as finely woven as their modern counterparts. Cotton was used for the warp and weft threads and an excellent-quality wool for the pile. Older

KNOT
asymmetrical

WARP
cotton or silk

WEFT
two shoots, cotton or silk

PILE
short, excellent-quality
wool or silk

ENDS
narrow kelim with long,
plain fringe at both ends

SIDES
single cord, overcast with
wool or silk

NAIN
◆

KNOT
asymmetrical

WARP
cotton or silk

WEFT
two shoots, blue cotton
or silk

PILE
short, excellent-quality
wool or silk

ENDS
kelim with knotted fringe
at both ends

SIDES
single cord, overcast
with wool

◆

Isfahan rugs tend to be more colorful with richer, deeper tones than the newer Isfahans. The Medallion, Tree, and Vase designs are commonly woven.

Carpets currently woven in Isfahan are considered the finest in Iran. Those of the best quality are made with silk warp and weft threads and an excellent quality of kork wool for the pile. Small amounts of silk are used to accentuate designs and motifs. All-silk rugs are also woven.

The workshops of Serafian, Daradashti, and Haghighi have earned reputations for producing rugs of a superb quality. Rugs from these workshops bear their inscriptions in a small cartouche in the minor border or kelim. These fine-quality Isfahan rugs are very expensive.

A wide variety of designs are woven in Isfahan, the most common of which is a multilobed jewel medallion super-imposed on a vine- and palmette-filled field, with four spandrels. The main border usually contains a palmette and leaf pattern. The color combinations are of blue, beige, and taupe. Isfahan rugs are woven in all sizes.

NAIN The town of Nain is located at the western edge of the desert, 90 miles (144 kilometers) east of Isfahan. Rugs from here are among the finest woven in Iran, with a weave that is comparable to the best of the antique carpets. The making of hand-knotted carpets in Nain began only in the 1930s. For centuries the town had been known for the weaving of fine woolen cloth used to make robes (*abas*), for mullahs, Muslim clerics. When the import of Western fashions and fabric brought about a decline in the cloth-weaving industry, the looms were converted to the manufacture of fine handwoven carpets.

Most Nain rugs are woven with cotton warp and weft threads and a fine quality of wool for the pile. Silk is often used to accentuate designs and motifs. All-silk rugs are also woven. The finest-quality Nains (*shish-la*) are woven with six-ply cotton used for the warps. The more coarsely knotted Nains (*no-la*) are woven with nine-ply cotton warps.

The finest Nain rugs are woven in the master workshops of the city itself, and those of coarser quality, in small outlying villages. In recent years the workshop of Habibian has become

ISFAHAN, 5' X 8'

NAIN, 6'6" X 9'9"

BACK OF ISFAHAN

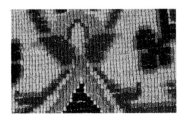

BACK OF NAIN

synonymous with fine-quality Nains. Rugs from this workshop have a signature inscribed in a small cartouche in one of the minor borders.

Designs of Nain rugs are intricate and finely executed. The pile is trimmed quite short, yielding motifs that are sharp and crisp. The most common design used in Nain is a medallion superimposed on a field filled with vines and palmettes. Prayer, bird and animal, and trellis designs are also woven.

The color palette used in Nain rugs is limited. A dark indigo blue, medium blue, beige, and shades of brown are the colors most commonly used. White silk is used to accentuate certain designs and motifs. The background color of Nains is usually blue or beige and less frequently red.

The quality of Nain rug weaving varies and, as can be expected, the price varies with the quality of the carpet. The finest-quality Nains are expensive. All sizes are woven, from small mats to room-size rugs.

BACK OF KASHAN

KASHAN

◆

KNOT
asymmetrical

WARP
cotton, silk

WEFT
two shoots,
dyed blue cotton or silk

PILE
medium short, excellent-
quality wool or silk

ENDS
alternating red and blue
yarn stitched across a narrow
kelim, knotted at both ends

SIDES
single cord, overcast
with wool

◆

KASHAN The town of Kashan is situated at the edge of the desert about 150 miles (290 kilometers) south of Tehran on the old caravan route from Tehran to Yezd and Kerman. For centuries Kashan has been renowned for the weaving of fine carpets. The carpet-weaving industry, like that of Isfahan, was severely damaged when the looms were burned during the Afghan invasion in 1722, and did not recuperate until the late 19th century.

A group of rugs known as Motasham Kashans, woven during the last part of the 19th century, have become highly sought after by collectors and quite expensive. These rugs are of excellent quality and very finely woven. Their designs are more stylized than those normally associated with Kashan rugs woven today.

Kashan had been a primary producer of silk carpets until recently when silk rugs from Qum began to dominate the Iranian silk rug market. Kashan silk rugs were woven with silk pile as well as silk warp and weft threads. Some Kashan silk rugs have wefts of blue dyed cotton.

The weaving of Kashan rugs is done within a 30-mile (50-kilometer) radius of the city. Kashan rugs are finely woven, although the quality does vary, with the finest-quality rugs being woven in the city itself.

A variety of designs are found in Kashan rugs, the most common being medallions and arabesques. Rugs with a central medallion have a field filled with floral sprays, vines, tendrils, and arabesques. Prayer rugs often have a Tree-of-Life or a vase, with emanating branches, vines, and tendrils, at the base of the field. Portrait and pictorial carpets are also woven.

Souf rugs are also made in Kashan. Rugs of this type are woven with a combination of a flat weave for the background and a knotted pile for the designs and motifs. Soufs may be woven either with cotton warp and weft threads and wool for the pile portion or with silk threads throughout.

Traditional colors of red and blue are used as well as soft pastels—beige, ivory, light blue, and a gray green. Kashan rugs come in all sizes. Prayer, portrait, and pictorial carpets are woven in a small format, about 4 by 6 feet, whereas medallion and arabesque designs range from small mats to large gallery sizes.

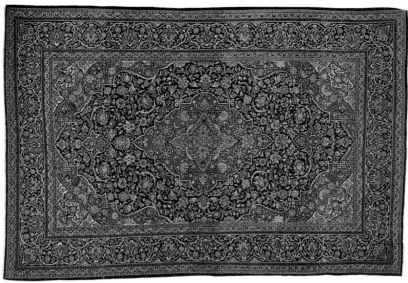

KASHAN, 4'4" X 6'6"

JOSHAGHAN The small town of Joshaghan is 75 miles (120 kilometers) north of Isfahan in the Kul-i-Varganeh valley. Rugs have been woven here for more than several hundred years and have changed very little in structure and design during that time.

The typical Joshaghan pattern consists of a field filled with an arrangement of diamond-shaped Gul-i-Henna, Mina Khani, and *Bid Majnun* (Weeping Willow) motifs. A diamond-shaped navy blue medallion is superimposed on the field with medium blue spandrels in the corners. The background is red with blue, white, yellow, and green used for the different motifs in the field. The main border is navy blue.

Joshaghan rugs are woven with good-quality wool and are very durable. A variety of sizes are made, from 3 feet 3 inches by 5 feet (100 by 150 centimeters) to room size.

The town of Meimeh, 11 miles (17 kilometers) west of Joshaghan, produces rugs which are identical in design to those of Joshaghan but are more finely woven and have a slightly shorter pile.

VISS (VIZ) Viss rugs are woven in the small town of Viss, near Khonsar, at the southern edge of the Arak region. The design most associated with these rugs is a hexagonal medallion

JOSHAGHAN, 4' X 6'   VISS, 5' X 7'

VISS

◆

KNOT
asymmetrical

WARP
cotton

WEFT
one shoot, cotton

PILE
wool, medium long

ENDS
knotted fringe at both ends

SIDES
single cord, overcast
with wool

◆

superimposed on a blue field, with spandrels. The colors used in Viss rugs are limited; blue and tomato red are the primary colors and small amounts of tan and yellow are used in the motifs.

The wool used is a good-quality, soft, lustrous wool. The rugs are inexpensive and durable. A variety of sizes are woven, from small mats to 9 feet 9 inches by 13 feet (3 by 4 meters).

CHAHAR MAHAL VA BAKHTIARI

Chahar Mahal va Bakhtiari is a small mountainous province wedged between the provinces of Isfahan, Fars, and Khuzestan. Shahr-e-Kord is the capital and the market center for Bakhtiari rugs woven by the nomads as well as by those woven in the small villages and towns of the province.

BAKHTIARI   Bakhtiari carpets are woven in numerous villages in a large area southwest of Isfahan called the Chahar Mahal. They are woven by Armenian, Kurdish, Turkic, and

BACK OF JOSHAGHAN

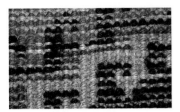

BACK OF VISS

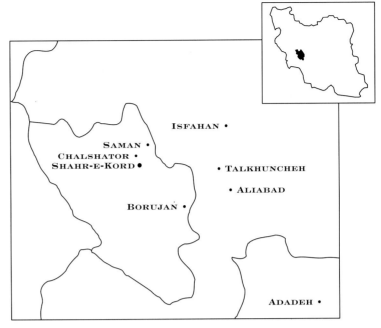

ISFAHAN •

SAMAN •
CHALSHATOR •
SHAHR-E-KORD •

• TALKHUNCHEH

• ALIABAD

BORUJAN •

ADADEH •

CHAHAR MAHAL VA BAKHTIARI PROVINCE

BAKHTIARI

◆

KNOT
symmetrical

WARP
cotton

WEFT
single or double; wool,
blue or undyed cotton

PILE
wool

ENDS
plain fringe at both ends

SIDES
single cord, overcast
with wool

◆

Persian villagers as well as Bakhtiari tribes. Isfahan serves as the major market center for carpets of this area.

The most common designs woven in Bakhtiari rugs are the Medallion, Panel, and Lozenge designs. The field of the Panel design is divided into rectangular compartments, each of which contains one of a variety of motifs: flowers, trees, boteh, or palmettes. This design was adopted from the matrix formed by the irrigation channels in Persian gardens. The lozenge design is similar to the Panel in that the field is segmented by repeating lozenges. Each lozenge contains a small motif similar to those used in the Panel design. This design is commonly found in older and antique Bakhtiari carpets.

The Medallion design is composed of a large lozenge-shaped medallion superimposed on a field filled with stylized floral patterns. Another type of Medallion design is that of a large stylized floral bouquet, referred to as a Gul-i-Franc, which is contained within a medallion.

The colors of Bakhtiari carpets can vary from somber with a predominant use of browns and rust-red tones to very bright

BAKHTIARI, 4' X 6'

with pink, white, and orange. The colors found in antique Bakhtiari carpets are mellow with rich, deep shades of red, blue, green, and white.

Bakhtiari carpets can vary greatly in quality. The finest-quality ones are woven in the village of Chalshator. These rugs are finely woven with cotton warps and a single wool weft. Rugs from Shahr-e-Kord are slightly less finely woven, with cotton warps and two shoots of wool weft. They have a stiffer handle and are not as supple as the Bakhtiari rugs from Chalshator. Saman rugs are not as finely woven as those from Shahr-e-Kord. They have a thicker pile and are stiffer to the touch.

In general the heavy wool used in Bakhtiari carpets is very durable and ideal for heavy traffic. Modern Bakhtiari carpets are woven in all sizes: room size, small rugs, and runners.

LURI The Lurs reside primarily in the provinces of Luristan, Khuzistan, and Fars. A small group of Lurs are settled near the city of Veramin. Luri carpets are woven by nomadic Lurs as well as by those Lurs who reside in villages and small towns.

Luri carpets produced by nomads are woven on horizontal

looms by women who also spin their own wool. The warps and wefts are of wool. The designs woven in Luri rugs often are influenced by the neighbors. For example, Luri rugs woven in the north near Kurdistan resemble Kurdish rugs; those woven in the south resemble the Qashqa'i rugs. Luri rugs tend to be more loosely woven than those of the Qashqa'i.

One of the most commonly used designs was that of three latch-hooked central medallions on a field packed with small motifs, such as boteh, animal heads, stars, and rosettes. A trellis pattern filled with eight-pointed stars or floral motifs is also found. Luri weavers are known for their use of animal motifs and their interpretation of latch-hook motifs which resemble bird heads, often with horns and eyes. The rosette-and-vine design on a white background is commonly used for one of the borders. The color palette of Luri carpets tends to be dark, with somber shades of brown, red, and blue.

The Luri also weave salt bags, saddlebags, storage bags, and kelims. Their rugs are usually woven in an elongated format, for example, or 5 by 9 feet (150 by 275 centimeters) to 6 by 12 feet (180 by 365 centimeters).

BACK OF LURI

LURI, 5' X 9'

BACK OF YELEMEH

YELEMEH, 5' X 9'

YELEMEH

KNOT
symmetrical or asymmetrical

WARP
wool or cotton

WEFT
one or two shoots, dark-
brown wool or cotton

PILE
medium-long soft,
lustrous wool

ENDS
knotted fringe at both ends

SIDES
single cord, overcast
with two colors of
wool yarn alternating in
diagonal stripes

◆

YELEMEH Yelemeh rugs are woven in numerous villages between Abadeh and Shiraz by Persian villagers and Qashqa'i tribes, and in the Chahar Mahal village of Borujan and the villages of Talkhuncheh and Aliabad in Isfahan Province. The type of knot used in Yelemeh rugs depends on whether the rug was woven by Persian villagers or Qashqa'i. Persian villagers use the asymmetrical knot and the Qashqa'i use the symmetrical knot.

Yelemeh rugs are colorful with beautiful shades of green, blue, yellow, orange, beige, red, and blue. Natural dyes are still used in most Yelemeh rugs.

The design most commonly used is that of three diamond-shaped latch-hook medallions reminiscent of Qashqa'i and Luri motifs. These medallions are placed on a field filled with a variety of small geometric motifs. Another design used is that of a field divided into either square or diamond-shaped compartments.

Yelemeh rugs are woven in a soft, lustrous good-quality wool. The best-quality rugs are woven in Aliabad, Borujan, and Talkhuncheh by the Qashqa'i. They are usually woven in smaller sizes up to 7 by 10 feet (210 by 305 centimeters).

FARS

The Fars province is a large area of rugged mountains and flat plains. It extends from Khuzistan in the west to Kerman in the east, from Isfahan on the north to the Persian Gulf on the south. The area is inhabited by numerous nomadic groups, including Qashqa'i, Khamseh, Lurs, and Arabs. Weaving in Fars is done by nomads, sedentary nomads, and Persian villagers. Shiraz, the capital and the largest city, is the major marketplace for rugs woven in the region.

SHIRAZ In many of the villages east of Shiraz, rugs of similar quality and design are woven by Arab and other Khamseh weavers. These rugs are labeled as "Shiraz." The differences between Persian village rugs and those woven by recently settled nomadic tribes are often hazy since there is frequently intermarriage between the villagers and the nomads of the same plain or valley.

Shiraz rugs are woven with geometric designs, rectilinear pole medallions, and repeated hexagonal motifs. The field usually contains a variety of small geometric motifs such as

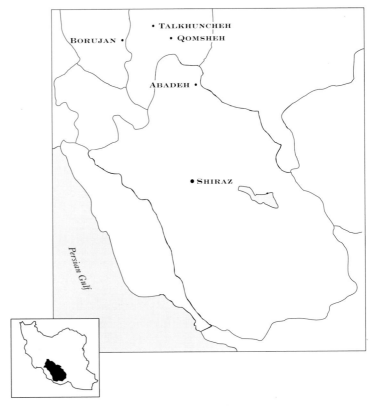

FARS PROVINCE

SHIRAZ, 4'3" X 6'

BACK OF SHIRAZ

birds, animals, and human figures. Shiraz rugs are woven with wool warp and weft threads; goat's hair is often mixed with wool in the warps. The sides are overcast either with goat's hair or two strands of alternating colored wool, giving a barber-pole effect. The medium-long wool pile has a soft texture. The colors are bright red, black, yellow, orange, white, and light and dark blue. The background is usually red with a dark blue or black central medallion and spandrels.

QASHQA'I   The Qashqa'i is the largest tribal group in southwest Iran. It is made up of five large tribes and numerous smaller tribes. Their territory extends from Abadeh and Shahreza in the Isfahan province to the Persian Gulf. Traditionally they are nomads, herders who migrate between winter and summer pastures in the highlands and lowlands of the Zagros Mountains. The men and boys care for the sheep; the women and girls do the spinning and weaving. It is common to see women tending to chores with wool in hand and spindle in tow.

Today, in addition to the nomadic way of life, the Qashqa'i also live in villages and towns. Men have jobs and women do weaving in their homes. The wool used is supplied or purchased and can be either naturally or chemically dyed. Both natural and chemically dyed wool can be used in the same rug.

QASHQA'I, 5' X 8'

Qashqa'i carpets are usually woven on horizontal looms. Often two women work side by side on the same loom, without a pattern, the design being reproduced from memory. Wool, goat's hair, or a mixture of both is used for the warp and weft threads. Goat's hair is also used to overcast the sides of the carpet.

The most common design is that of a dark-blue central medallion and spandrels on a red field, which is filled with small birds, animals, human figures, and geometric and floral motifs. Other designs commonly used by the Qashqa'i include three connecting pole medallions, vertical stripes, and repeated boteh. Red and blue are the primary colors. White, orange, yellow, blue, and green are used for the numerous motifs scattered throughout the field. Qashqa'i rugs are woven in a variety of sizes from 2 by 3 feet (60 by 90 centimeters) to 8 by 10 feet (245 by 305 centimeters).

In addition to the weaving of pile carpets, Qashqa'i women also weave animal trappings, saddlebags, kelims, and *jajims* as well as a variety of other objects for household purposes, such as salt bags and storage bags. The Qashqa'i also weave Gabbehs.

BOWNAT Rugs known as Bownats are woven by Arab Khamseh, who reside in the villages east of Shiraz. Bownat rugs are similar to the Qashqa'i and Shiraz rugs in design and color. They have a dark-blue or black geometric central medallion and spandrels on a red background. Bownat rugs are woven with either cotton or wool warps and dark-colored wool wefts. Green is used frequently in the motifs, much more than in the Qashqa'i or Shiraz rugs. Bownats are woven with a thicker, denser pile than Qashqa'i rugs and are slightly more expensive.

GABBEH Gabbeh rugs are woven by nomads in the Zagros Mountains region of Fars. The majority of weaving is done by Qashqa'i or Luri weavers. Gabbehs are usually woven on horizontal looms by women and young girls, who also spin and dye much of their own wool.

Traditional Gabbeh rugs are coarsely knotted with numerous weft threads between each row of knots. The pile is a long shaggy wool. Rugs are small and tend to be squarish.

BACK OF GABBEH

GABBEH, 7' x 7'

GABBEH

◆

KNOT
asymmetrical or symmetrical

WARP
light- or dark-brown wool,
or a mixture of both

WEFT
wool, dyed red

PILE
wool; thick, long pile

ENDS
kelim turned under and
stitched to the back of the
carpet; or a small kelim with
knotted fringe or
braided fringe

SIDES
terminal warp threads
overcast with one or two
colors of wool

◆

Modern Gabbeh rugs, made for markets in the West, are woven with thick, coarse knots and a relatively long pile. Two to four weft threads are used between each row of knots. Because of their dense pile, Gabbehs of this type withstand wear much better than their earlier counterparts.

The designs used are simple geometric patterns. The most common is that of a central medallion or several medallions on a large expanse of open field. Small geometric motifs, birds, animals, and plants are scattered throughout the field. Other designs are also woven, such as a central stylized tree, lions, zigzag stripes, and bands.

Gabbehs are colorful, with bright shades of golden yellow, red, orange, blue, green, and white. Some Gabbeh rugs are woven with natural, undyed wool in shades of beige, brown, and black and others with a mixture of undyed and brightly colored wool. Gabbeh rugs woven by Qashqa'i weavers are more colorful and have a more uniform weave than those of Luri weavers, whereas Luri Gabbehs contain designs that are more varied and free-form in nature.

Gabbehs are occasionally made with pile on both sides and a different design on each side. These "double-sided" Gabbehs, called *patuee*, are used as mattresses and blankets.* This type of Gabbeh is loosely woven and floppy.

Most Gabbeh rugs tend to be squarish in shape, in sizes from 4 by 5 feet to 7 by 9 feet. Recently larger sizes up to 9 by 12 feet have been woven for the North American market.

ABADEH Abadeh is a small town situated about halfway between Isfahan and Shiraz. The weaving of carpets for export began in Abadeh after World War II.

The designs used in Abadeh rugs have been adopted from various tribal groups who made their summer camps in the area. The most common is that of a red geometric medallion which expands to fill a large portion of the field. The lozenge-shaped medallion contains a small central geometric rosette, which is also repeated in the four large corner spandrels. Stylized Tree-of-Life motifs emanate from the center rosette and the spandrels, and numerous small geometric motifs are interspersed throughout the field and medallion. The primary colors are red, blue, and white. Small amounts of yellow and green are used for the small motifs in the field.

ABADEH

◆

KNOT
asymmetrical

WARP
cotton

WEFT
two shoots, cotton,
dyed light blue

PILE
short, good-quality wool

ENDS
narrow kelim with plain or
knotted fringe at both ends

SIDES
single cord, overcast
with wool

◆

ABADEH, 7' X 10'

*Parviz Tanavoli and S. Amanolah, *Gabbeh: G.D. Bornet Collection 2* (Baar, Switzerland: Georges Bornet, n.d.) p. 23.

YEZD

◆

KNOT
asymmetrical

WARP
cotton

WEFT
three shoots, cotton,
dyed blue

PILE
wool

ENDS
knotted fringe at both ends

SIDES
one cord, overcast
with wool

◆

Another design used in Abadeh rugs is the Zil-i-Sultan design, characterized by vases of roses repeated in rows throughout the field. In Abadeh, this design is usually woven on a white background.

The warp and weft threads are of cotton. The wool used for the pile is an excellent quality and these rugs are quite durable. The pile is trimmed short, yielding designs which are crisp and clear. Most Abadeh rugs are woven in small sizes up to 4 feet 6 inches by 7 feet (135 by 210 centimeters) and short runners approximately 2 feet 6 inches by 6 feet 6 inches (75 by 200 centimeters).

YEZD (YAZD) The city of Yezd is the capital of and largest city in the Province of Yezd. It is located halfway between Kerman and Isfahan. The weaving of knotted carpets in Yezd has been documented as early as the 17th century and has always been on a relatively small scale.

The most common design in Yezd rugs woven before 1920 was a large-scale Herati pattern. In newer Yezd rugs the most common design is a central floral medallion on an open field or with detached floral sprays. The spandrels are filled with bouquets of flowers. Modern Yezd carpets resemble the rugs of Kerman in their structure.

Red and blue are the most common background colors, with ivory, yellow, and shapes of pink and blue occurring in the motifs. The wool is from the Kerman area and is very durable. Yezd rugs are woven primarily in large and room-size formats. Few Yezd carpets have been exported to North America, although they are common in European and Iranian markets.

KERMAN PROVINCE

The Kerman province is the third largest province in Iran. The Dasht-e-Lut occupies the northeast portion of the province; much of the rest of the province is composed of sandy desert and steppe. The city of Kerman is the capital and largest city; it also serves as the marketplace for Afshari and Kerman rugs in the province.

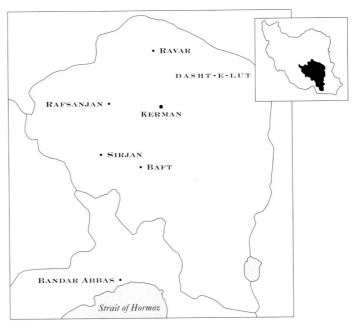

KERMAN PROVINCE

KERMAN

◆

KNOT
asymmetrical

WARP
cotton, depressed

WEFT
two or three shoots,
light-blue cotton

PILE
medium to medium long
in length

ENDS
knotted fringe at both ends

SIDES
single cord, overcast with
wool the same color as
the ground

◆

KERMAN (KIRMAN) The city of Kerman is located 660 miles (1,064 kilometers) southeast of Tehran. Carpet weaving has been done in Kerman since the 16th century, although the rug industry remained on a relatively small scale until the late 19th century. Currently weaving is done in Kerman and the surrounding villages.

During the last several decades of the 19th century, a large number of pictorial rugs were woven, depicting a shah, or ruler, enthroned, mythological heroes, portraits, and pastoral landscapes. Other designs from this period were adopted from Kerman shawl patterns. After World War I, patterns such as repeated medallions or a central medallion with palmettes and arabesques filled the background. The overall tone of the rug was darker; dark-blue backgrounds were commonly used with red, green, ochre, and light blue in the designs.

After World War II, designs were inspired by French Aubusson carpets. These rugs are woven with a dense, thick pile. The designs are composed of a central floral medallion on either an open field or a field with detached floral sprays. A broken border design, consisting of swirls of flowers, was used instead of the traditional squared corner border arrangement.

BACK OF KERMAN

KERMAN, 6' X 6'

Pastel colors were used for the floral motifs; ivory, rose, light blue, and pale green were common backgrounds. Kermans of this type were intended for the American market, and became known as "American Kermans." Kermans made for the Persian market during this period were also characterized by a central floral medallion and an open field. They were more finely woven and had a shorter pile.

All sizes of rugs are woven, from small mats to large gallery-size carpets; runners and occasionally round rugs are woven.

Ravar (Lavar, Laver). Some of the finest Kerman rugs have been attributed to the small village of Ravar, located 84 miles (140 kilometers) north of Kerman. In Europe and North America the name has been corrupted to Lavar. For years the weavers in Ravar were renowned for their excellent-quality rugs. Unfortunately, in recent years the quality has deteriorated.

AFSHAR The largest weaving population of the Afshar tribe resides in the Kerman province in southeast Iran. The

KNOT
symmetrical or asymmetrical

WARP
wool or cotton

WEFT
two shoots, brown or dyed
red or blue wool; one or two
shoots, dyed red, orange,
pink, or blue cotton

PILE
wool, medium

ENDS
wide decorated kelim in
older rugs and plain fringe at
both ends in newer rugs

SIDES
one cord, overcast with
bands of different-
colored wool or overcast
with wool
◆

Afshar area is to the south and southwest of the city of Kerman, in and around the towns of Sirjan, Rafsanjan, and Baft. Sirjan is the largest weaving center for Afshar carpets.

Afshari rugs are woven by nomads and villagers whose lifestyle is very similar to that of the Qashqa'i and Persian villagers of Fars. In villages, Afshari rugs are woven on both horizontal and vertical looms with asymmetrical knots and cotton warps and wefts. They are more finely woven and have a thicker body and stiffer feel than those woven by the nomads. Nomadic rugs are woven on horizontal looms and are symmetrically knotted with wool warps and wefts. These rugs have a much looser, floppier feel.

A variety of designs are used in Afshari weaving, such as the Zil-i-Sultan, countered rows of boteh, diamond-shaped medallions, and the *morgi* design. Some Afshari designs show a Kerman and urban influence; others are traditional Afshari patterns. The *morgi* ("hen") pattern, for example, is an imaginative design that originated with the Afshars and has since been adopted in Fars and other areas in Iran.

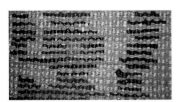

BACK OF AFSHAR

AFSHAR, 4' X 5'

Afshar rugs are usually small, rarely over 5 by 7 feet (150 by 215 centimeters), and tend to be squarish in shape. In addition to rugs, the nomads weave saddlebags, storage bags, salt bags, and horse covers. The Afshars also weave soumak carpets (see Chapter 14).

KHORASAN PROVINCE

Khorasan is an immense province which occupies the northeast quadrant of Iran. Much of it is remote and sparsely populated. Khorasan is one of the major wool-producing areas of Iran. Many different ethnic groups reside in Khorasan: Balouchi, Turkomans, Kurds, Arabs, and Persians. Each of these groups weaves rugs with characteristics that reflect the ethnic origin of the weaver. Mashad serves as the major marketplace for these rugs.

MASHAD Mashad, the capital and largest city in Khorasan, is a holy city sacred to Shiite Muslims. The shrine of Imam Ali Reza, a Shiite holy man who died there in A.D. 819, has attracted many pilgrims since the Safavid dynasty (1502–1736). The dynasty, which established Shiism as the Persian state religion, reached its height during the reign of Shah Abbas the Great

MASHAD

◆

KNOT
asymmetrical

WARP
cotton

WEFT
two or three shoots,
light-blue cotton

PILE
wool, excellent quality

ENDS
knotted fringe at both ends

SIDES
single cord, overcast
with wool

◆

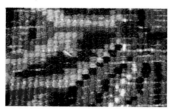

BACK OF MASHAD

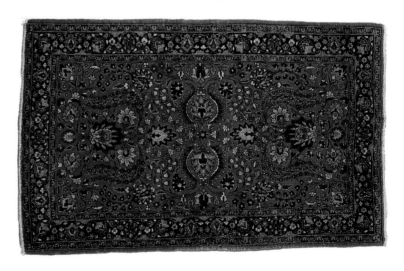

MASHAD, 4' X 6'

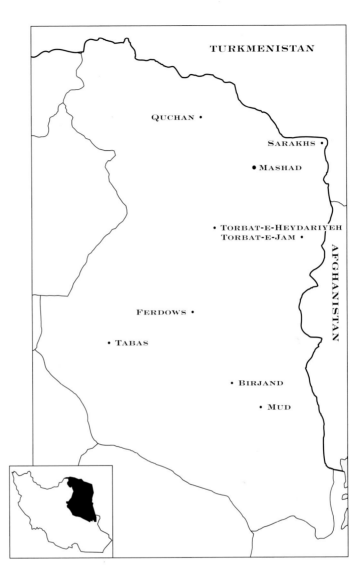

KHORASAN PROVINCE AND
WEAVING CENTERS

(1587–1629), who embellished the city with many fine buildings.

Mashad carpets are woven in the city of Mashad as well as in the 500 or more area towns and villages. The Shah Abbas design, on a burgundy or mauve background, is most commonly associated with Mashad rugs. The design may be used as an allover pattern or in conjunction with a central medallion. Blue, pink, ivory, yellow, green, and orange are used for the motifs.

The wool used for the pile is soft and lustrous. The pile is medium high and dense. Very fine-quality Mashad rugs frequently have their sides finished with a wide multicord

MUD, 6' X 6'

BACK OF MUD

MUD

◆

KNOT
asymmetrical

WARP
cotton

WEFT
cotton

PILE
wool, trimmed short

ENDS
small kelim with knotted
fringe at both ends

SIDES
single cord, overcast
with wool

◆

selvedge in silk or wool. The ends of Mashad carpets often are finished in multicolored bands. The last several rows of pile are knotted in 2- to 3-inch portions of yellow, green, orange, ivory, pink, and light and dark blue.

MUD (MOUD, MOUTE) The small town of Mud is located approximately 250 miles (400 kilometers) south of Mashad. Rugs woven in Mud vary from good to excellent in quality.

The Herati pattern on an ivory background is almost exclusively woven in Mud rugs. The Herati motif is employed either as a repeated pattern or in conjunction with a round jewel medallion and quarter-medallion spandrels. Shades of blue, green, and rose are used for the motifs. Hot pink, yellow, or turquoise silk is used as a highlight to accentuate certain designs and motifs. In very fine Mud rugs, white silk frequently is used to fill the background of the medallion and spandrels. The main

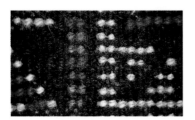

BACK OF QUCHAN

QUCHAN, 3'6" X 6'6"

border often contains a cartouche motif on a rust or blue background. The majority of Mud rugs are woven in large sizes.

QUCHAN Quchan is a small town situated about 80 miles (135 kilometers) northwest of Mashad near the border with Turkmenistan. The area is inhabited by Kurds as well as a large number of Turkomans who reside just to the north of Quchan. Rugs are woven in Quchan as well as the surrounding area.

Some of the designs used by the Kurdish weavers in Quchan resemble those used by Kurds in western Iran. Other designs resemble those used in Caucasian, Balouchi, and Turkoman rugs. The most common are small repeated latch-hook motifs, a single large latch-hook medallion, and a diagonal stripe pattern.

Quchan is a large wool-producing area with much of its production sent to other parts of Iran. The wool used in the less expensive Quchan rugs tends to have a bristly feel. These rugs are not finely knotted but should wear reasonably well. The colors used are somber: shades of brown, rust, tan, green, and gray.

Quchan rugs are small, 3 feet 3 inches by 6 feet 6 inches (1 by 2 meters) to 4 by 7 feet (120 by 180 centimeters).

BIRJAND The town of Birjand is located on the caravan route between Mashad and Zahedan, to the south. In general, the quality of rugs woven in Birjand is not as good as that of

QUCHAN

◆

KNOT
symmetrical

WARP
gray wool

WEFT
two shoots, dark brown or dyed red wool

PILE
medium-long wool

ENDS
small kelim with plain fringe

SIDES
single cord, overcast with wool or goat's hair

◆

BIRJAND

◆

KNOT
asymmetrical

WARP
cotton

WEFT
two shoots, cotton

PILE
wool

ENDS
knotted fringe at both ends

SIDES
single cord, overcast
with wool

◆

the rugs from Mashad and Mud. The weavers are known to use the jufti knot (see page 22). The Shah Abbas, Herati, and Boteh patterns are used. The background is frequently ivory. The majority of rugs are woven in large sizes.

TABAS   The town of Tabas is situated halfway between Mashad and Yezd. Rugs woven here resemble the rugs of Nain in their designs and color combinations. The central medallion on a field of vines, palmettes, and tendrils and a pattern of diamond-shaped motifs are commonly used. The colors are dark blue, gray blue, and ivory. Tabas rugs are not as finely woven as Nains and are less expensive. The majority of Tabas rugs are woven in small sizes up to 6 feet 6 inches by 9 feet 9 inches (2 by 3 meters).

BALOUCHI (BALUCHI, BELOUCHI) Balouchi tribes reside in eastern Iran, western Afghanistan, and the Balouchi province of Pakistan. In Iran, Balouchi weaving is centered in

TABAS, 3' X 5'

Khorasan Province around the towns of Torbat-e-Heydariyeh, 62 miles (100 kilometers) south of Mashad, and Torbat-e-Jam, 78 miles (130 kilometers) southeast of Mashad near the Afghan border. Numerous tribes and clans make up the Balouchi population in eastern Iran. Originally nomadic, many Balouchis now live a largely sedentary existence, engaging in pastoral activities.

Balouchi rugs are woven on a horizontal loom by women and young girls. The warp and weft threads are usually wool. In some villages, cotton is used for the warps. The wool used for the pile is of good quality and can be very lustrous in older rugs. Camel's wool occasionally is used in the pile.

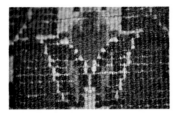

BACK OF TABAS

TABAS

◆

KNOT
asymmetrical

WARP
cotton

WEFT
cotton

PILE
wool; silk used as highlights

ENDS
knotted fringe at both ends

SIDES
single cord, overcast
with wool

◆

BALOUCHI, 3'5" X 5'

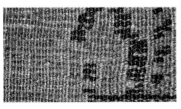

BACK OF BALOUCHI

BALOUCHI, 3' x 5'

BALOUCHI

◆

KNOT
asymmetrical

WARP
light-colored wool,
occasionally mixed with
goat's hair; cotton in
some new rugs

WEFT
one or two shoots, wool

PILE
wool, trimmed short

ENDS
wide kelim, often
decorated with a brocaded
motif and knotted fringe at
both ends

SIDES
two or more cords;
overcast with dark-brown or
black goat's hair or
horsehair or occasionally
braided

◆

The Balouchi are known for the weaving of small rugs, especially in the Prayer design. A classic Balouchi prayer rug is composed of a square prayer arch with a stylized Tree-of-Life motif in the field; flanking the mihrab, stylized depictions of open hands are placed in ivory panels. Many different motifs are used to fill the prayer niche.

Other patterns woven by the Balouchi include repeated guls, panels of latch-hooked motifs, zigzag bands, and diagonal stripes. The designs used are influenced by where the rug originated. Balouchi rugs woven in towns have more curvilinear designs than those woven by nomads. The Herati, Mina Khani, and Boteh patterns are frequently used in village weaving. Many Balouchi rugs have numerous narrow borders in red and black. The running-dog border is frequently used in Balouchi weaving.

Balouchi rugs from the town of Sarakhs are finely woven and have very curvilinear designs. The pile is trimmed short, yielding designs that are extremely crisp and clear. Depictions of animals and floral motifs are frequently woven. The Herati pattern was commonly used in older rugs with the colors green, blue, brown, and white.

The Balouchi palette is limited and the colors are somber. Shades of dark reddish brown, dark brown, blue, rust, orange, camel, and white are found. The brown wool in older rugs is often corroded.

They are woven in small sizes, 3 feet 3 inches by 5 feet (100 by 150 centimeters) to 4 by 7 feet (120 by 215 centimeters). In addition to small carpets Balouchi weavers make numerous bags for various uses, such as salt bags, *khorjin* (saddlebags), horse blankets, cushion covers, animal trappings, and *sofreh* (eating cloths).

Rugs woven by other ethnic groups such as Kurds, Arabs, or Timuri are similar to Balouchi rugs in structure and are often labeled as "Balouchi." Arab tribes around Ferdows weave rugs similar to Balouchi rugs in structure that are often called Balouchi.

KAZAK (LORI PAMBAK), 4'6" X 7'

six

RUGS OF THE CAUCASUS

aucasian rugs are woven in the mountainous Caucasus region, which lies within the republics of Armenia, Georgia, Azerbaijan, and the Autonomous Republic of Daghestan. This narrow strip of land, between the Black and Caspian seas, forms a land bridge between Europe and Asia. The Caucasus Mountains cross the area from northwest to southeast. The area to the south includes the weaving areas of Kazak, Karabagh, Shirvan, Talish, and Gendge; to the north are the Daghestan and Kuba weaving districts.

The Caucasus area is inhabited by numerous ethnic groups, with different languages and religions: Armenians, Georgians, Azerbaijanis, Kurds, Circassians, Leghianis, and Jews. As these peoples intermingled, designs from one area were adopted by another. For example, a diagonal stripe pattern found in Gendge also appears in the rugs of Kazak and Daghestan. Other designs remained associated with a specific village or area, such as Chelaberd, with its "Eagle" or "Sunburst" designs.

Traditionally Caucasian rugs were woven with wool pile, symmetrically knotted. The majority of rugs have wool warp and wool weft threads. The wefts pass two or more times between each row of knots. Caucasian rugs usually are woven with geometric designs and motifs.

Many Caucasian rugs have dates incorporated into the design of the rug. The dates may be based on the Islamic Hegira system, the Christian Gregorian system, or in some rugs both dating systems appear. (See page 43 for a conversion procedure.) Dates written in Arabic numbers usually are based on the Islamic calendar; those in Western numbers are based on the Christian calendar. Occasionally a Christian weaver used Arabic numbers while recording a date based on the Gregorian system.

Classic Caucasian rug weaving has given way to commercial factory production, with the result that modern Caucasian rugs have very little in common with their predecessors. In Armenia, Azerbaijan, and Daghestan weaving is now done in government factories and workshops and by individuals in their homes.

Kelims, soumaks, and other flat weaves were also traditionally woven in the Caucasus (see Chapter 14).

KAZAK

KNOT
symmetrical

WARP
natural colored wool,
three-ply

WEFT
two or more shoots of wool,
usually dyed red

PILE
long, thick, heavy wool

ENDS
looped fringe at one end;
braided fringe, turned
under and stitched
at the other

SIDES
two or three cords, wrapped
with red wool

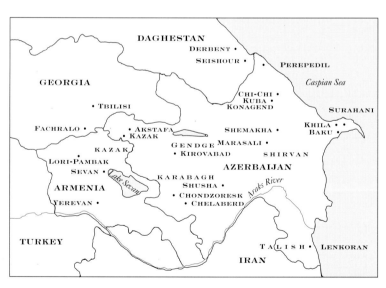

WEAVING AREAS OF THE CAUCASUS

SEVAN MEDALLION

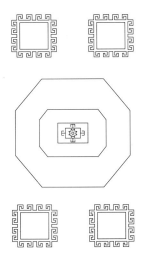

KARACHOP MEDALLION

KAZAK The Kazak weaving district is a large area composed of numerous small towns and villages in the southwestern part of the Caucasus. The area is inhabited primarily by Armenians, Azerbaijanis, and Kurds.

Kazak rugs are woven with bright colors and large-scale geometric designs. The field is often dominated by a single medallion or two or three medallions. The colors used are clear, bright, and contrasting; the color palette is composed of red, blue, white, yellow, and green. Kazak rugs have a medium knot count with a thick, relatively long, shaggy pile. Most rugs are woven in sizes 4 by 6 feet (120 by 182 centimeters) to 5 by 8 feet (150 by 244 centimeters).

Sevan (Sewan) Kazaks are woven along the northwest shore of Lake Sevan in Armenia. Sevan Kazaks are known for a large heraldic medallion on a red field. They are woven in relatively large sizes and tend to be squarish in shape. The primary colors used are red, blue, and white.

Lori Pambak rugs are woven in the town of Lori-Pambak and the surrounding area. Their design is composed of a large white octagonal medallion within which is a large cruciform terminating in a tulip form (see page 100). The field is red. A serrated leaf- and-wineglass design is often used in the main border. The primary colors used are red, white, and green.

Bordjalou rugs are woven in an area south of the Georgian city of Tbilisi. The designs of this area are characterized by a field compressed by a very wide main border, which is divided into reciprocal sections of latch-hook medallions. The field may be filled with latch-hook medallions or other rectilinear motifs. Bordjalou rugs tend to be squarish in shape. The primary colors used are red, blue, and white.

The design most associated with Karachop (Karachov) rugs is a large white octagonal medallion, encased in a square or larger octagon. Small squares or octagons similar to the central medallion are placed in each corner.

The Prayer design is frequently encountered in Fachralo rugs. Within the prayer niche, the field is dominated by an eight-pointed star medallion which has a rather flattened shape. The medallion is white and encases a smaller similar red or green medallion.

**MEMLING GUL
MEDALLION**

BACK OF GENDGE

GENDGE

◆

KNOT
symmetrical

WARP
ivory-colored wool

WEFT
three or more shoots; wool,
usually dyed red

PILE
wool, medium long

ENDS
looped fringe at one end,
knotted at the other

SIDES
two or three cords, wrapped
with wool

◆

GENDGE, 4' X 7'   **KAZAK (FACHRALO), 4' X 6'**

GENDGE (ELIZAVETPOL, KIROVABAD) Rugs
known in Oriental rug literature as "Gendge" were woven in
and around Kirovabad, halfway between the Black and Caspian
seas, in an area inhabited primarily by Armenians and
Azerbaijanis. Due to its strategic location on caravan routes and
later as a railway center, Gendge became a collection center
for the rugs of Kazak, Karabagh, and Shirvan, as well as Gendge.

The designs woven in Gendge rugs tend to be smaller-
scaled than those woven in Kazak. The designs most associated
with Gendge rugs are repeated boteh or octagons, diagonal
stripes, and a lattice pattern. Rows of repeated octagons,
containing Memling Guls, may fill the field. The stripe pattern
is composed of multicolored diagonal bands, each of which
contains a series of small boteh, stars, or small hooked motifs.
In lattice pattern rugs the framework is filled with stars or floral
forms. Gendge rugs are colorful with bright shades of red,
yellow, blue, white, and green.

Gendge rugs occur in small sizes, approximately 4 feet by
8 feet 3 inches (120 by 250 centimeters), and in an elongated
format, approximately 3 feet 3 inches by 11 feet 6 inches (100
by 350 centimeters).

◆

KNOT
symmetrical

WARP
light-colored wool, three-ply

WEFT
two or more shoots of brown
wool, occasionally dyed red

PILE
wool, medium long

ENDS
looped at one end, braided
and turned under at the
other

SIDES
two or three cords
wrapped with wool

◆

**CHONDZORESK
MEDALLION**

KARABAGH (KARABAKH) The Karabagh district lies southeast of the Kazak district in the southern part of the Caucasus along the border with Iran. It is inhabited primarily by Armenians and Azerbaijanis. The major villages of the Karabagh district include Chelaberd, Chondzoresk, and Shusha.

Many different designs are woven in Karabagh rugs. Repeated boteh, single and multiple medallions, bouquets of roses, Herati, and prayer designs are common.

Chondzoresk rugs also known as "Cloudband Kazaks" are woven. Their design is composed of two octagonal medallions on a red field. At the center of each octagon is a square, frequently containing a swastika-type motif. Encompassing the octagon are stylized dragon or cloudband motifs. The field is decorated with small rosettes, stars, and other geometric motifs. The main border commonly contains the serrated leaf-and-wineglass design.

Chelaberd rugs are also described in the literature as "Sunburst" or "Eagle Kazaks." The design associated with these rugs contains one or two radial medallions on a red background. Each medallion consists of a cross superimposed on a diamond shape; from the cross, rays emanate into the field. A stylized rosette design on a white field is often used for the main border.

Kassim Ushak are recognized by their large cruciform medallions, within which is a smaller, diamond-shaped medallion. Two wide white bands bracket the top and bottom of the medallion. Within the brackets is an abstract motif which is probably the remains of a degenerated dragon form. A large number of Kassim Ushak rugs contain Armenian inscriptions. The main border consists of either the serrated leaf-and-wineglass or a rosette design.

Lampa rugs are woven in two basic designs. One has an alternating lobed medallion and elongated rectangular medallions on a dark-blue field, with pairs of confronting birds on either side of the medallions. The other design is composed of diamond-shaped medallions outlined by a wide magenta serrated band. The Lampa rugs are woven in runner sizes, 3 feet 3 inches by 16 feet 3 inches (100 by 500 centimeters).

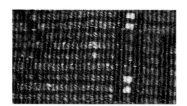

BACK OF KARABAGH

KARABAGH, 5' x 8'

CHELABERD MEDALLION

KARABAGH (KASSIM USHAK), 6'4" x 8'

LAMPA MEDALLION

TALISH Talish rugs are woven in the southeast portion of the Republic of Azerbaijan. The Talish district is bordered on the north by the Araks River, on the south by Iran, on the west by Karabagh, and on the east by the Caspian Sea. The area is inhabited by Azerbaijanis, Kurds, Shahsavans, and Armenians. Lenkoran is the largest city of the region.

BACK OF TALISH

TALISH

◆

KNOT
symmetrical

WARP
wool

WEFT
two shoots, dark-brown or
dyed-red wool, cotton, or a
mixture of both

PILE
silky wool, medium long

ENDS
small kelim with plain fringe

SIDES
two or three cords,
wrapped with blue wool

◆

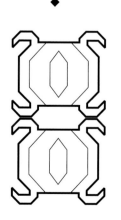

LENKORAN MEDALLION

TALISH, 3' X 6'6"

The design most associated with Talish rugs is that of a long, narrow center field and a relatively wide main border. The field, outlined with a zigzag motif, may be empty, decorated by a single design element, or have small rosettes and stars scattered randomly throughout. In addition, a repeated design of rosettes or eight-pointed stars and lattice pattern encasing floral or boteh motifs are also woven in Talish rugs. The main border is composed of large stylized rosettes flanked by small geometric floral forms on a white background. The outer border usually contains a reciprocal, arrow-type pattern, known as *medachyl*. Blue is the most common background color, although red and ivory are also used.

A characteristic feature of Talish rugs is their long, narrow format. Common sizes are from 3 feet 3 inches by 7 feet (100 by 200 centimeters) to 3 feet 3 inches by 8 feet (100 by 240 centimeters); however, longer rugs are woven.

The rugs woven in Lenkoran are structurally similar to those woven in other areas of the Talish district. However, they vary in the type of design employed. The classic Lenkoran design is composed of three or more octagons flanked by stylized dragon forms. Lenkoran rugs tend to be longer than other rugs woven in the Talish area. Their most common sizes are from 3 by 8 feet (90 by 244 centimeters) to 3 feet 6 inches by 9 feet (106 by 274 centimeters).

SHIRVAN The Shirvan weaving district lies south of Kuba along the southeastern slopes of the Greater Caucasus mountain range. During the late 19th century the population of this area

K n o t
symmetrical

W a r p
wool, three-ply (two brown
and one white)

W e f t
white or natural-colored
wool or cotton

P i l e
wool, cut short

E n d s
small kelim with plain
fringe at both ends

S i d e s
two cords, wrapped with
white cotton (occasionally
blue wool)

◆

BACK OF SHIRVAN

was primarily Azerbaijani, although Armenians and Russians also inhabited the area.

Rug production from the Shirvan weaving district has been prolific. A variety of designs are woven, such as single or multiple medallions, prayer, trellis, and repeated small geometric motifs.

The structural features characteristic of Shirvan rugs include the three-ply wool used for the warp threads. Two strands of dark wool are plied with one strand of white, or two strands of white with one strand of dark brown. The warp threads also are on the same plane, giving a flat appearance to the back of the rug, compared with the ribbed backs of Kuba and Daghestan rugs. The sides of Shirvan rugs are usually two cords wrapped with white cotton, as compared with Kuba rugs, which are usually wrapped with blue wool. Some Shirvan rugs, however, have their sides wrapped with blue wool.

The design most associated with the village of Marasali is a stylized prayer arch with a field filled with repeated multicolored botehs. The Marasali boteh is unique in that it

SHIRVAN, 3'5" x 4'5"

AKSTAFA, 3'5" X 9'9"

has a serrated outline. White or yellow often is used for the background color. The main border is often composed of a Boteh and Meandering Vine design on a white background or stylized, interlocking botehs. In some borders the boteh has evolved into a bird form. These rugs are finely woven with a soft, lustrous wool. Marasali rugs tend to be small and squarish in shape.

AKSTAFA The village of Akstafa is located within the Kazak weaving district, halfway between Kirovabad and Tbilisi. Rugs known as Akstafa, however, are more similar structurally to the rugs of Shirvan rather than Kazak.

The classic Akstafa design is composed of a series of alternating red and white eight-pointed star medallions flanked by large fan-tailed birds on a dark-blue background. The field is full of small geometric motifs, birds, camels, other animals, and human figures. The primary colors used are blue, white, and red; turquoise is used occasionally.

Akstafas are usually woven in an elongated format, 3 feet 3 inches by 7 feet 3 inches (100 by 220 centimeters) to 4 feet by 9 feet 9 inches (120 by 300 centimeters).

KUBA Rugs known as Kuba are woven in the town of Kuba and numerous small villages in the Kuba district. The Kuba weaving area is bordered by Daghestan on the north and Shirvan on the south.

A wide variety of designs are woven in Kuba rugs, such as prayer rugs, Herati, radial medallions, a ram's head motif, repeated rows of stepped polygons, and a trellis pattern. Certain designs have become associated with the names of various villages where they are alleged to have been woven. Whether or not these designs were actually woven in these villages or in several villages throughout the district has been the subject of some debate. The most famous of these villages are Chi-chi, Perepedil, Seishour, and Konagend.

One of the distinguishing features of Kuba rugs is the slightly ridged appearance of the back of the rug. This is a result of the slight depression of the warp threads. Another distinguishing feature is the several rows of blue soumak

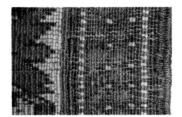

BACK OF KUBA

KUBA (PEREPEDIL), 3'5" x 4'9"

KUBA

◆

KNOT
symmetrical

WARP
light-colored wool, two- or
three-ply

WEFT
two shoots, light-colored
wool or cotton

PILE
wool, cut short

ENDS
several rows of blue
soumak stitching followed
by multiple rows of knots
and plain fringe

SIDES
two or three cords,
wrapped by
blue wool

◆

stitching between the pile portion of the rug and the rows of knotted fringe.

Chi-chi rugs are characterized by a field somewhat compressed by series of elaborate borders. The field is filled with repeated rows of small stepped polygons. The background is usually blue with red, yellow, blue, green, and white motifs. The main border contains repeated crosses or floral forms separated by a diagonal bar on a white background. Other borders have multicolored diagonal stripes and small repeated flowers. Chi-chi rugs are small and squarish in shape.

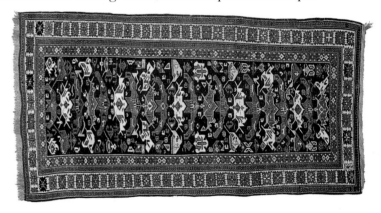

KUBA, 5' x 9'6"

The design most often associated with the Perepedil rugs is a central octagon or star burst flanked by ram's head motifs. The main border is composed of a white Kufic design on a dark-blue background.

Characteristic of the Seishour (Seichur, Sejour, Zeykhur) rugs is a vertical series of large Saint Andrew's crosses which dominate the field. Stylized floral motifs are used to fill the expanses. The main border contains a design resembling the running-dog border. Seishour rugs are usually woven in an elongated format.

Two types of designs are associated with Konagend rugs, that of a large central medallion with four smaller square medallions in the corners of the field, and a central field covered by a white trellislike pattern on a blue background.

KONAGEND MEDALLION

BAKU Baku, the capital of the Republic of Azerbaijan, is located on the Apsheron peninsula in the Caspian Sea. The villages of Surahani and Khila are included in the Baku area and are associated with certain designs. The weaving from these villages, like that of Baku, is very similar in structure to that of Shirvan.

The Boteh design is most often associated with the rugs of Baku. The colors tend to be more muted than those of other areas of the Caucasus. Rugs from this area are noted for the shades of blue and turquoise used. A multicolored diagonal

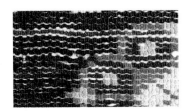

BACK OF BAKU

BAKU (KHILA), 3'6" X 5'

BAKU

◆

KNOT
symmetrical

WARP
light-colored wool; cotton

WEFT
two shoots; cotton,
light-colored wool, or a
mixture of both

PILE
wool, medium short

ENDS
looped fringe at
one end, knotted fringe
at the other

SIDES
one cord, wrapped in
light-colored wool
or cotton

◆

stripe design and a repeated carnation design are commonly used in the minor borders.

The designs associated with Khila are a medallion and spandrels on a blue background which is filled with repeating rows of boteh, and a medallion flanked by four large rosettes on a blue background. Red and white rays often emanate from the medallion and spandrels. The sizes vary from 3 feet 3 inches by 5 feet (100 by 150 centimeters) to 4 feet by 9 feet 3 inches (120 by 280 centimeters).

The weavers of Surahani are known for their use of octagonal medallions. A design frequently used is that of vertically placed octagonal medallions outlined by a wide white band referred to by Ian Bennett as a Garden design.*

Two or three octagons, representing little islands, are enclosed within stylized pools linked by channels. The weavers of Surahani are known for the use of turquoise color. Currently adaptations of traditional designs are woven in Surahani by large carpet factories. The sizes typically woven are 6 feet 6 inches by 9 feet 9 inches (2 by 3 meters) and smaller.

MODERN CAUCASIAN RUGS

Modern Caucasian rugs are woven in Azerbaijan, Armenia, and Daghestan. Armenian weaving is done in Yerevan and in towns north and west of Lake Sevan. In Azerbaijan the greatest concentration of weaving is in the Baku area. Daghestan weaving is centered around Derbent. The weaving is done in large factories, workshops, and by individuals in their homes.

The quality of modern Caucasian rugs is determined by the number of knots per square meter. The quality grades are given the names of towns and regions; however, there is no relationship between the two. For example, Van-quality rugs are woven in Yerevan and Kamo, not in Van.

Modern Caucasian carpets are woven with cotton warp and weft threads on vertical steel looms. These looms are able to maintain an even warp tension during the weaving process,

*Oriental Rugs, vol. I, Caucasian (London: Oriental Textile Press, 1980), p. 220.

MODERN CAUCASIAN

◆

KNOT
symmetrical

WARP
cotton

WEFT
two shoots, cotton

PILE
wool, medium

ENDS
small kelim with knotted fringe at both ends

SIDES
two cord, overcast with wool

◆

QUALITY GRADE	KNOTS PER SQUARE METER	KNOTS PER SQUARE INCH
AZERBAIJAN CARPETS		
Kuba-Shirvan	250,000	161
Kazak	120,000	77
ARMENIAN CARPETS		
Shirvan or Van	250,000	161
Yerevan	160,000	103
Kazak	120,000	77
DAGHESTAN CARPETS		
Mikrakh	250,000	161
Derbent	160,000	103

ensuring that the rug will have straight sides and lie flat. Old Caucasian rugs were woven with wool warp and weft threads on more primitive looms and are frequently irregular in shape.

Traditional Caucasian designs from Khila, Perepedil, Seishour, Chondzoresk, and Afshan are woven, and new patterns are being developed. Rectilinear medallions and repeated geometric motifs are frequently used.

Chrome dyes are used, which are colorfast; they will not fade when exposed to sunlight or bleed when washed. The colors in modern Caucasian rugs are stronger than the mellow tones of their antique counterparts. The rugs of Armenia are given a light chemical wash before export; those from Azerbaijan and Daghestan are not. After export, some rugs are given a stronger "antique" wash in Europe.

Caucasian carpets come in a variety of sizes ranging from small mats to 6 feet 6 inches by 9 feet 9 inches (2 by 3 meters). Larger sizes are available as well as runners. In addition to pile carpets, soumaks are also woven (see Chapter 14).

The majority of modern Caucasian rugs are sent to markets in Europe. They are available in North America but in relatively small numbers.

MODERN CAUCASIAN RUG (SHIRVAN QUALITY), 5' X 8'

TEKKE, 3' X 4'

seven

TURKOMAN AND AFGHAN RUGS

Turkestan is a politically undefined area in Central Asia. It extends from the Caspian Sea on the west to the Gobi Desert in China on the east and from the Kazakh steppe in the north to the Kopet-Dagh, Hindu Kush, and the Paropamisus mountain ranges in the south. Turkestan is divided into Western and Eastern Turkestan by the Tien Shan mountain chain. Western Turkestan encompasses northeast Iran, northern Afghanistan, and Turkmenistan. Eastern Turkestan lies within the Autonomous Region of Xinjiang in China (see Chapter 9). The Turkoman peoples who reside in this area are descendants of the Oghuz and are of Turkic stock. They are divided into tribes and numerous subtribes.

The Russian conquest of Turkestan began in the 17th century. By the middle of the 19th

century, most of western Turkestan had come under Russian control. In the 1880s the last Tekke tribe was defeated by the Russians. Eastern Turkestan was under Chinese rule for most of the 19th century.

Traditionally the Turkomans lived a nomadic and seminomadic existence, residing in large round tents called *yurts*. They migrated freely, unaffected by political boundaries. This lifestyle changed for many Turkomans when the Soviet Union began to strictly enforce their borders in the 1930s. They were no longer free to migrate where they chose. During this time some Turkomans left their traditional homeland and moved to Afghanistan and Iran.

Weaving was done by women and young girls on horizontal looms. The women spun their own yarn and dyed their own wool. The wool used was from their own herds. The patterns used were from memory, learned as a child. Turkoman women also wove numerous utilitarian pieces for use in their daily life.

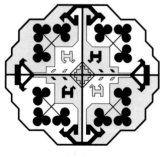

GUL-I-GUL

The pattern most associated with Turkoman weaving is that of rows of repeated geometric motifs, or *guls*, woven on a red background. This small octagon motif is a tribal emblem, which was once unique to a specific tribe or subtribe. Guls were primarily used on carpets and *chuvals* (storage bags). Smaller bags, tent bands, animal trappings, and other weavings

SALOR

◆

KNOT
asymmetrical

WARP
thin, light-colored wool, deep
warp depression

WEFT
one or two shoots, light-
colored wool

PILE
short, tightly knotted, fine-
quality wool

ENDS
kelim with plain fringe

SIDES
two to four cords,
overcast with dark-blue
or red wool

◆

contained other types of designs. The *ensi*, or door cover, is composed of a *hatchli* (cross) design. The field is divided into quadrants by perpendicular broad stripes. Within each of the quadrants are small repeated motifs.

Turkoman rugs have been referred to as "Bukharas." Bukhara, now in Uzbekistan, was a collecting point and market for Turkoman rugs to be shipped to the West. In the past, due to a lack of knowledge of the tribal origin of these rugs, they were often called "Bukharas."

RUGS OF TURKESTAN

SALOR One of the oldest Turkoman tribes, the Salors were also once the wealthiest and most prestigious, but tribal wars and disputes have dispersed their population. By 1870, many Salors had been absorbed into the Sariq and Tekke tribes. The Salors occupied the oasis area surrounding Merv from the late 17th century until driven from their homelands by the Tekke tribe in 1856. A small group of Salors still reside around Marutshak in northern Afghanistan.

Two types of guls are used in Salor weaving: the *gul-i-gul* and the *turret gul.* The gul-i-gul is an octagonal motif containing a smaller polygon, divided into quadrants. It is similar to the gul used by the Ersari. The outer quadrant also has branches, which terminate into the three round cloverlike motifs at each end of the branch. This type of gul was often used in main carpets. The turret gul is an octagonal motif with spiked projections that point both inward and outward from its rim. A smaller octagon appears at the center of the gul. The turret gul is often employed on the faces of storage bags. The secondary guls used in Salor rugs resemble the major guls of the Tekke and Sariq tribes.

The colors used in Salor rugs vary from a brilliant red to a dark purple-red. The Salors used the finest-quality wool, and their weaving technique was the best of all the Turkoman tribes. Small amounts of magenta-colored silk were used in the guls.

The Salors wove main carpets, approximately 9 by 12 feet (270 by 370 centimeters), and storage bags of various sizes. Salor carpets are among the rarest of the Turkoman rugs.

SARIQ GUL

SARIQ

◆

KNOT
symmetrical, occasionally
asymmetrical

WARP
wool, alternating warps
slightly depressed

WEFT
two shoots, gray wool

PILE
medium short, wool

ENDS
wide kelim with plain fringe
at both ends

SIDES
two cords overcast with
alternating dark-blue and red
wool, giving a checkered
appearance

◆

A Salor-like turret gul is woven in Afghanistan by members of the Sariq tribe. The rugs in which these guls appear resemble the traditional Sariq rugs in colors and skirt ornamentation, and are sold as Sariq Mauri.

SARIQ (SARYK, SARIK) The Sariq are an old but rather small Turkoman tribe. Since the late 19th century, groups of them have resided along the Murghab River south of Merv (in the Pinde district), around Marutshak, and between Maimana and Qaisar.

The classic Sariq gul is composed of an octagon, similar to that of the Tekke. The gul is generally divided into quadrants of alternating colors, with the center of the gul containing a crosslike motif. The secondary guls resemble those used by the Tekke. Members of the Sariq tribe also use the turret gul in their bags.

Sariq rugs woven after 1880 were deep purplish brown, darker than those made by most Turkoman tribes. Earlier Sariq weaving contains lighter colors. Magenta silk and white cotton are occasionally used in the guls.

The Sariq wove main carpets and storage bags of various sizes. The Sariq torbas and chuvals have a dark-blue plain edge at the top of the bags and long blue fringes.

TEKKE The Tekke tribe is the largest and most important of the Turkoman tribes. They reside between the Caspian Sea and the Amu Darya River in Turkmenistan, and in Iran near Bujnurd and Gonabad in Khorasan.

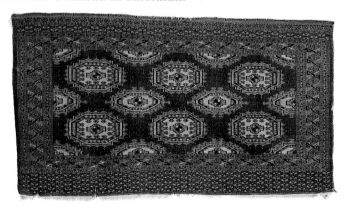

SARIQ CHUVAL, 2'6" X 5'

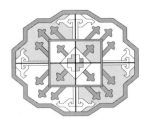

TEKKE GUL

CHEMCHE GUL

KURBAGE GUL

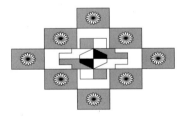

SAGDAK GUL

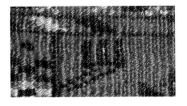

BACK OF TEKKE

The Tekke gul is an octagonal motif divided symmetrically into quadrants. Each gul contains an eight-pointed design (six-pointed in newer rugs) emitting spiked projections. The guls are connected to neighboring guls by horizontal and vertical lines which run through the field of the carpet (see page 114). Secondary or minor guls occupy the space between the rows and columns of the major Tekke guls. The *chemche* (spiderlike) and the *kurbage* guls are secondary guls most often used in Tekke rugs. The *sagdak* secondary gul is frequently used in Tekke chuvals.

Three borders generally surround the field of the rug. The main border contains a series of octagons enclosing star motifs. At the top and bottom of a Tekke rug, outside the borders, is a wide panel containing a different design. Called an *elam* or skirt, this usually contains a hooked diamond motif. Ground colors vary from brick red to a dark wine red. White, burnt orange, and dark blue are used in the motifs.

The field of the Tekke *hatchli* is divided into quadrants by two perpendicular strips or bars, resulting in a crosslike form. Within each of the quadrants is a candelabra-like motif. At the top of the cross an arch may be present. In this type of design, the skirt is present only at the bottom of the rug.

In addition to carpets, the Tekke also wove numerous chuval, torba, and mafrash storage bags with designs usually different from those woven in carpets. A common pattern for bags is a field that has been divided into compartments, each of which contains a small gul.

Tekke rugs and bags are woven with wool warp and weft threads. They are finely woven, with warps on the same level. Both loops of the knot are equally visible. This is possible because of the thin weft used between the rows of knots and the thin yarn used for the knots. In Tekke weaving there are twice as many knots in length as in width in a given area; for example, 20 knots in length as compared to 10 knots across.

In Turkmenistan, Tekke rugs are woven in standardized sizes, ranging from small mats to room-size rugs. In Iran, primarily small sizes up to 4 by 6 feet (120 by 180 centimeters) are woven.

Tekke-design rugs are woven not only by members of the

TEKKE

KNOT
asymmetrical

WARP
ivory or light-brown-colored
wool

WEFT
two shoots,
light-colored wool

PILE
short, fine-quality wool

ENDS
bands of kelim, striped
or decorated with
embroidered motifs

SIDES
two cords, overcast with
navy blue wool, occasionally
red wool

Tekke tribe but by numerous other Turkoman tribes as well. The Tekke gul is used in Iran by Yomuds, in Afghanistan by Sariq and Ersari, in Pakistan, and in India.*

YOMUD (YOMUT) The Yomud, one of the largest Turkoman tribes, is composed of many subtribes that have become widely scattered. Groups of them live in northeastern Iran, around Khiva, along the eastern shores of the Caspian Sea in Turkmenistan, and in northwest Afghanistan.

In Yomud rugs the two guls most frequently used are the *kepse* and *dyrnak* guls. Both have an elongated lozenge shape; the kepse is outlined with latch-hooked edges and the dyrnak has serrated edges. The Yomud residing in Iran also weave a Tekke-like gul in addition to their traditional Yomud gul. At the ends of Yomud rugs between the borders and the kelim are wide bands of piled area called a *skirt* or *elam*. These skirts contain a variety of different motifs.

The *hatchli* design, woven by the Yomud, is composed of a field divided into quadrants by wide stripes. Each of the quadrants is filled with small repeated diamond-shaped motifs. In this type of design the skirt is present at the bottom only. The chemche gul is frequently used by the Yomud in chuvals

*Pakistani and Indian rugs with Turkoman gul designs are referred to as "Bukharas."

DYRNAK GUL

KEPSE GUL

YOMUD, 3'5" x 5'3"

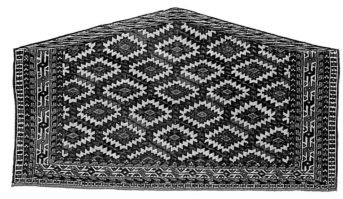

YOMUD OSMALYK, 2'6" X 5'

KNOT
asymmetrical and
symmetrical

WARP
wool or goat's hair

WEFT
two shoots (single in new
Iranian Yomuds), gray wool

PILE
wool, short to medium short

ENDS
wide kelim with either
braided or plain fringe

SIDES
two cords, overcast
with wool

◆

and other bags. Yomud chuvals commonly have a wide undecorated band at the bottom of the bag.

The reds used in Yomud rugs vary from reddish brown to a wine red. White is used as the background for the primary border. The Yomud tend to use a larger amount of white than other Turkoman tribes. In addition to the use of white, yellow, green, blue, and brown are commonly used in Yomud rugs.

The Yomud were prolific weavers of saddlebags, storage bags, tent bands, tent pole bags, horse blankets, kneepads for camels, and a variety of other animal trappings and storage bags in different sizes and shapes. The *osmalyk*, a five- or seven-sided trapping, is used to decorate the flanks of a camel during a bridal procession.

YOMUD ENSI, 4' X 5'

BACK OF YOMUD

ERTMEN GUL

CHODOR

◆

KNOT
asymmetrical

WARP
dark-brown wool

WEFT
two shoots; wool, cotton, or a
mixture of both

PILE
long wool, coarsely woven

ENDS
kelim with plain fringe

SIDES
four cords, overcast
with two colors of wool in
a check pattern or with
goat's hair

◆

TAUK NOSKA GUL

CHODOR The Chodor are a relatively small tribe who reside in Turkmenistan. One group inhabits an area north of Khiva and another group lives north of Beshir.

In Chodor weaving, the *ertmen* and the *tauk noska* guls are the most frequently used. The *ertmen* gul is an elongated, stepped hexagonal emblem that is generally placed within a lattice framework. This use of a lattice pattern is unique in Turkoman weaving. On bags and animal trappings, the ertmen gul appears as a half-gul or in combination of complete and half-gul motifs; the lattice framework is also used. The octagonal *tauk noska* gul is divided into quadrants, each of which contains a pair of double-headed animal motifs. Prayer rugs and *hatchli* design rugs are also woven by the Chodor.

Chodor weaving is coarse compared to that of other Turkoman tribes. The field color varies from light purple to violet brown. White cotton occasionally is used to accentuate certain motifs. The main carpets are woven in the 6 foot 6 inch by 9 foot 9 inch (2 by 3 meter) format and larger.

ERSARI The Ersari tribe is the largest Turkoman population in Afghanistan and also the principal rug-weaving group. It is composed of many subtribes that reside in a large area between Andkhoi and Mazar-i-Sharif. During the war in the 1980s, many Ersari left their homeland and became refugees in Pakistan. Since that time many have become active in rug weaving in Pakistan.

The principal guls woven in Ersari rugs are the *gul-i-gul*, *tauk noska*, and *temirchin*. The gul-i-gul woven by the Ersari is an octagon motif, encompassing a polygon. The outer quadrant contains three trefoil motifs which extend from a center polygon. The tauk noska gul is an octagonal motif divided into quadrants, each of which contains at least one pair of a stylized doglike motif. In later rugs this motif has evolved into an H motif. The temirchin gul also is an octagonal motif, divided into quadrants. At the center is a square containing a floral motif. Each of the outer quadrants contains a horizontal, serrated, spearheadlike motif.

The Ersari *hatchli* is composed of a field that has been divided into quadrants. Each of the quadrants is divided into

ERSARI

◆

KNOT
asymmetrical

WARP

gray-colored wool or goat's
hair, little or no warp
depression

WEFT
two shoots, dark-colored wool
or goat's hair

PILE
thick, long, excellent-quality
wool

ENDS
wide red kelim decorated
with bands of gray or brown
stripes, with knotted fringe at
both ends

SIDES
three or four cords, overcast
with dark-brown wool or
goat's hair

◆

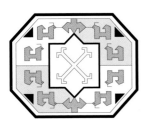

TEMIRCHIN GUL

BACK OF ERSARI

segments which contain a plantlike motif. The colors used in the background vary from red to a deep maroon. Ersari frequently use yellow and green in their rugs. The white used in designs in often cotton, as the Ersari had little access to white wool. They breed Karakul sheep, which have dark-colored wool. Ersari carpets have the lowest knot count of Turkoman rugs and are more coarsely woven. They also have the longest pile. The sides of Ersari rugs are finished with multiple cords, and the terminal warps are overcast with either goat's hair or wool.

Ersari rugs are woven primarily in large sizes, 6 feet 6 inches by 9 feet 9 inches (2 by 3 meters) and larger. In addition to main carpets, the Ersari wove numerous storage bags in various sizes.

ERSARI ENSI, 4' X 5'6"

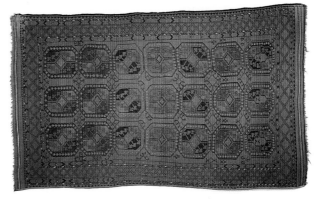

ERSARI, 9' X 13'

The Ersari have resided in northern Afghanistan for several hundred years. Other Turkoman tribes moved into Afghanistan at different periods to escape Russian oppression and enforced controls on their way of life. The latest wave of migration occurred in the 1930s. Many of the Turkomans were Tekke from the Merv area who resettled in and around Herat.

Turkoman and Balouchi weavers are responsible for the greatest volume of carpets produced in Afghanistan. Other tribal groups, including Uzbek, Pashtun, and Chahar Aimak, also weave carpets, but their total output is smaller.

Traditional Turkoman patterns and colors are among the patterns most frequently woven in Afghanistan. After World War II, new designs and adaptations of traditional tribal patterns began to appear in Afghan rugs. The majority of carpets are woven with wool pile and wool warp and weft threads. Both local Afghan and imported Australian wool are used in carpet weaving. Much of the local wool is spun by hand. Cotton and silk are occasionally used for the warps. Silk pile rugs are also produced, but this output is relatively small.

AFGHAN, 7'9" X 10'6"

AFGHAN PURDAH, 4' X 5'

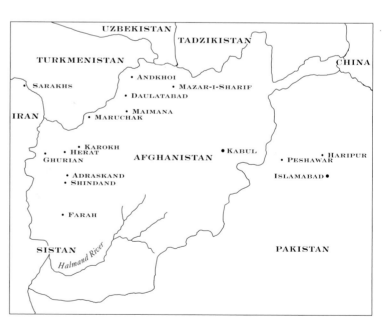

MAJOR WEAVING AREAS OF AFGHANISTAN

KNOT
asymmetrical

WARP
light-colored wool

WEFT
one or two shoots, dark-
colored wool

PILE
short, evenly trimmed wool

ENDS
wide kelim with knotted
fringe at both ends

SIDES
two cords, overcast
with dark-blue or
black wool

◆

Natural and chemical dyes are used in Afghanistan. Some rugs contain a combination of both types. In vegetable dyeing, madder is used for red, indigo for blue, and isparak for yellow. The black or charcoal-colored wool is often undyed.

Traditionally carpets were woven by women and girls in their homes. The weaving was done on a horizontal loom with a mother and her daughters working side by side. Once workshops were established in the cities, carpet weaving was done by young men and boys.

MAURI Mauri carpets are of excellent quality and finely knotted. They are woven primarily by Tekke, Sariqs, and Ersari in Maruchak, Mazar-i-Sharif, Herat, and other villages and towns in northern Afghanistan. The majority of Mauri rugs are woven with the Tekke gul. Mauri rugs with a Salor-type turret gul, a Sariq skirt design, and Sariq colors are woven by a group of Sariqs residing north of Herat.

The Zaher Shahi design, developed after World War II, is also used (see page 129). This design is composed of hexagonal, lozenge-shaped guls interconnected by a series of bands. These rugs are usually woven with a white background with red, green, orange, and camel used for the pattern.

Purdah and Prayer designs are frequently woven in this quality. In Afghanistan the *ensi*, or door covering, is known as a *purdah*, which means curtain. It was used to cover the door of the yurt. Purdahs are woven with fringe on the bottom end only.

MAURI BACK

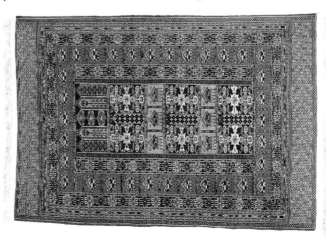

MAURI, 4' X 6'

KNOT
asymmetrical

WARP
gray wool

WEFT
two shoots, red or
dark-colored wool or one
cotton and one wool

PILE
thick, heavy wool

ENDS
wide kelim with knotted
fringe at both ends

SIDES
two cords, overcast
with wool

♦

DAULATABAD, 3' X 5'

The top is woven with a kelim band which is turned under and sewn to the back of the carpet. Purdahs were woven with various shades of red for the background, with dark blue, black, and white for the pattern. During the 1970s purdahs were made with gold-colored backgrounds and shades of brown and ivory for the motifs. Purdahs are very finely woven, with pile that has been trimmed quite short. The majority of these rugs are woven in small sizes, although larger sizes are now being made for use on the floor.

DAULATABAD The town of Daulatabad is located in the Faryab province, halfway between the towns of Maimana and Andkhoi. The majority of rugs from this area are woven by Turkomans and Uzbeks. Prayer rugs with red backgrounds are frequently found. Gold and small amounts of ivory are used for the motifs.

Daulatabad is also used as a trade name for good-quality rugs woven in various weaving centers in northern Afghanistan. Daulatabads have a thicker pile and are not as smoothly trimmed as Mauris. Most Daulatabads are woven by Ersari tribes with one of their guls. The most commonly used guls in Daultabad weaving are the *taghan, suleiman,* and *dali* guls. The octagonal taghan gul is divided into quadrants within each of which are several elongated pronged motifs. The dali gul is a gul-i-gul. The suleiman gul is an enlarged copy of the temirchin gul.

AFGHAN WAR RUGS During the early 1980s, coinciding with the military presence of the former Soviet Union in Afghanistan, rugs from Afghanistan began to appear with military motifs. Tanks, assault rifles, grenades, MiG fighter planes, helicopters, and personnel carriers were woven in knotted pile rugs as well as in flat weaves. Similar rugs were also woven in Pakistan by Afghan refugees.

The early "war rugs" had motifs inconspicuously placed within the traditional patterns; however, within a few years the war theme often dominated the pattern. The field design consisted of alternating rows of helicopters and tanks or a large Kalashnikov rifle with small grenades interspersed throughout the field. Repeated tank motifs were used as the main border design.

TAGHAN GUL

AFGHAN WAR RUG,
3'3" X 6'

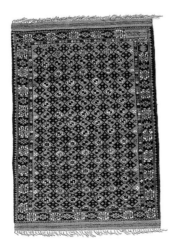

AFGHAN REFUGEE RUG,
4' X 6'

The palette included combinations of a blue background with green, brown, and white motifs or a camel or ivory background with red, orange, black, and brown motifs. The majority of these rugs were woven in small sizes, 3 feet by 4 feet 6 inches (90 by 140 centimeters) to 4 by 7 feet (120 by 215 centimeters).

AFGHAN REFUGEE RUGS Many Afghans left their homeland to live in refugee camps established in Pakistan after the Soviet army occupied Afghanistan in 1979. Since the early 1980s many of these camps in northern Pakistan have evolved into villages and towns.

Carpet weaving is the major means of support for the refugees in Pakistan. The Turkomans make up the largest weaving population, although other ethnic groups also produce carpets. Weaving is done by boys and young men as well as by women. Traditionally among the Turkomans, weaving was a task done only by women and girls.

Many of the early refugee carpets were crudely woven with poor-quality wool and dyes that were not colorfast. However, since the early 1980s the quality of refugee rugs has greatly improved. Rugs are currently woven in different qualities, with good dyes and excellent-quality wool. The wool used comes from Afghanistan, Pakistan, and Australia. Many of the rugs contain a mixture of both Pakistani and Australian wool. Australian wool has a softer, more lustrous texture.

In northern Pakistan, numerous Afghan carpets can be found in the markets. Some of these rugs are old; others are recently woven. The greatest number of these carpets have traditional Turkoman designs, although Caucasian and Persian patterns are also found. These copies are well executed with designs that are crisp and clear.

Rugs are woven in a variety of sizes. In addition to carpets, storage bags in various sizes, saddlebags, bicycle seat covers, and coasters are also woven.

In the Haripur refugee camp, the Ersari Turkoman Project produces rugs woven with traditional Turkoman designs, using wool from Afghanistan that is hand-spun in Pakistan. The dyes used are vegetable: indigo for blue, madder for red, and isparak

AFGHAN

REFUGEE

◆

KNOT
asymmetrical

WARP
wool

WEFT
two shoots, wool

PILE
thick wool

ENDS
wide kelim with knotted
fringe at both ends

SIDES
single cord of terminal
warp threads, overcast with
brown goat's hair

◆

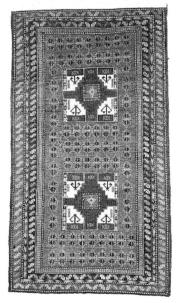

BALOUCHI (SISTAN),
4' X 6'

for yellow. The rugs are not chemically washed or artificially aged. They will acquire a natural patina with time.

The Ersari Project carpets have a medium weave with a rather thick pile. The colors used are limited to three shades of blue, brown, dark peach, red, pale yellow, and ivory. A variety of sizes are woven.

BALOUCHI Balouchi rugs are woven in western Afghanistan along the border with Iran, from the Sistan area in the south to Sarakhs in the north. The Balouchi in Afghanistan comprise several tribes and subtribes that lead a largely seminomadic existence. Women and young girls do the weaving on horizontal looms. The Chahar Aimak and other ethnic groups weave rugs that are similar to those of the Balouchi and are often sold under the Balouchi name.

Balouchi rugs woven in Afghanistan are similar to those from Iran. They have wool warps and wefts and their colors are dark and somber. Shades of brown, purple, charcoal, aubergine, dark red, and dark blue are commonly used. The majority of rugs are woven in small sizes, approximately 3 feet 6 inches by 6 feet 6 inches (110 by 200 centimeters). The Balouchi also weave storage bags, pillows, animal trappings, eating cloths, and various other items for household uses.

A wide variety of designs are woven by the Balouchi in Afghanistan. Repeated geometric motifs, prayer rugs, picture rugs with stylized human figures, Tree-of-Life, and a concentric diamond pattern are all commonly woven. Many of these designs can be attributed to certain areas and tribes.

The *Mushwani* tribe resides west of Herat near the village of Ghurian and north near Karokh. Their rugs tend to be dark and somber with designs composed of highly stylized motifs. They weave numerous bags, small carpets, and kelims. The carpets have a wide decorated kelim at both ends. A pattern used by the Mushwani is that of concentric diamond shapes, outlined with serrated or latch-hook edges.

The *Dokhtar-i-Ghazi* tribe reside north of Herat and weave prayer rugs with a pointed mihrab and a field filled with small repeated motifs. The colors are usually limited to red, blue, black, and small amounts of white in the borders.

BALOUCHI

◆

KNOT
asymmetrical

WARP
ivory-colored wool,
occasionally mixed with
goat's hair

WEFT
two shoots, black
or gray wool

PILE
wool

ENDS
elaborately decorated
kelim with knotted fringe;
occasionally a second
multicolored fringe added

SIDES
as many as five cords, overcast
with goat's hair

◆

Adraskand is located about 40 miles south of Herat. Several different types of medallions are woven in this area, including a palmette-type medallion and a medallion composed of leaf motifs. Stylized human figures are also woven in this area.

The *Sistan* area lies along the banks of the Halmand River in southern Afghanistan. Weaving here is done by several Balouchi groups. The rugs from this area tend to be lighter in color than Balouchi rugs woven in the north. Designs woven in this area include stylized human and animal figures, square medallions, repeated motifs, and prayer rugs.

Koudani rugs are woven in the Herat area. These rugs are finely woven in the prayer design, with a square mihrab on an ivory or caramel-colored field filled with a stylized Tree-of-Life.

BALOUCHI (MUSHWANI),
2'6" x 4'6"

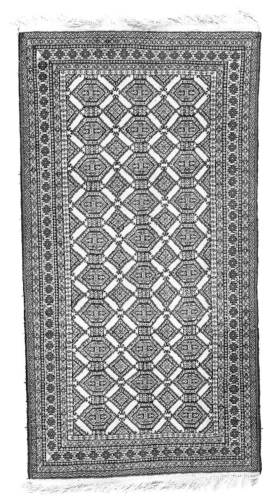

BALOUCHI (ZAHIR SHAHI), 3' x 6'

HEREKE (SILK), 2' X 3'

eight

RUGS OF TURKEY

ugs from Turkey were among the first Oriental rugs to reach Europe, where they were known as "Turkey carpets." Turkish carpets were first depicted in European paintings in the early 14th century, in the works of the Sienese and Florentine schools. During the Renaissance, such artists as Memling, Van Eyck, Bellini, Holbein, Lotto, and Carpaccio depicted Turkish carpets in their Madonna and Child paintings. Carpets can also be seen hung from windowsills, balustrades, and parapets, as well as draped over tables.*

The majority of the people living in Turkey are ethnic Turks. Kurds who reside in eastern Turkey constitute the largest ethnic minority, and there are small populations of Armenians, Greeks, and Jews, with the Greek population residing primarily along the west coast.

*Janice S. Herbert, "Oriental Rugs in Western Painting, Part I," *Oriental Rug Review* IV: 6 (September 1984), 2–3.

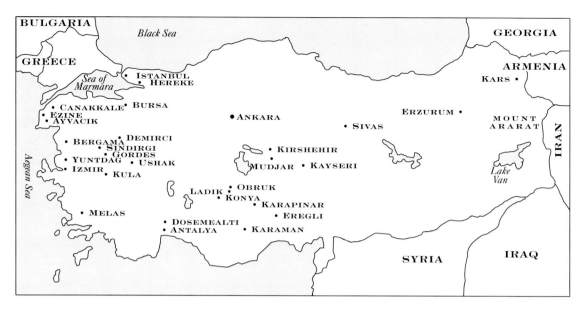

RUG-WEAVING CENTERS
OF TURKEY

BACK OF HEREKE SILK

Until the 1920s there was a large Armenian population in eastern Turkey, where they were responsible for weaving large numbers of rugs in Sivas, Kayseri, Kirshehir, Kars, Erzurum, and numerous other towns and villages. Armenians also were involved in weaving in Hereke and the Kum Kapu district of Istanbul. Some Armenian rugs have dates and inscriptions discreetly placed within the overall design of the rug.

Vast numbers of prayer rugs were woven in Turkey over the past several hundred years. Each weaving area or town had its own style and type of prayer design. Unlike Caucasian and Persian prayer rugs, Turkish prayer rugs usually have a panel at the top or bottom of the field.

Animal and human motifs are rarely depicted in Turkish rugs. The majority of Turks are Sunni or orthodox Muslims, who adhere to the Koran's prohibition against depicting human and animal forms.

For centuries Turkey has had an agricultural economy. After the Turkish Republic was proclaimed in 1923, Kemal Ataturk, its first president, began to remake and modernize the country. He abolished the use of the Arabic alphabet and replaced it with a modified Western one. Islam was removed as the state religion, Turkish names were given to cities, and a program of industrialization was begun. Even today, approximately half of the population still resides in rural areas. Carpets are still woven

KNOT
symmetrical

WARP
silk or cotton

WEFT
silk or cotton

PILE
silk or wool

ENDS
small kelim, often
decorated with small motifs
in knotted pile, with knotted
fringe at both ends

SIDES
single cord, overcast with
wool or silk

◆

in these areas in very much the same manner as has been done for hundreds of years.

Turkish rugs are named for the village or town in which they are woven. Carpets from very small villages often are called by the name of the town where they are marketed. Kurdish and nomadic tribal rugs are the exceptions. Kurdish rugs are sold by their tribal name; rugs woven by the nomadic tribes inhabiting the Anatolian Plateau are called Yuruks.

HEREKE Hereke, known as Anacircum by the Romans, is located at the eastern end of the Sea of Marmara, approximately 40 miles (65 kilometers) east of Istanbul. In 1843 an imperial factory was founded in Hereke to weave the finest-quality carpets for the Ottoman court. Hereke is still renowned for making some of the world's finest carpets.

Two types of carpets are woven in Hereke. One type has wool pile and cotton warp and weft threads; the other has silk pile and silk warp and weft threads. Wool-pile carpets are woven primarily in large sizes. The majority of silk rugs are woven in smaller sizes.

A variety of designs are woven in Hereke, many of which were adapted from those of Persian carpets. The patterns are

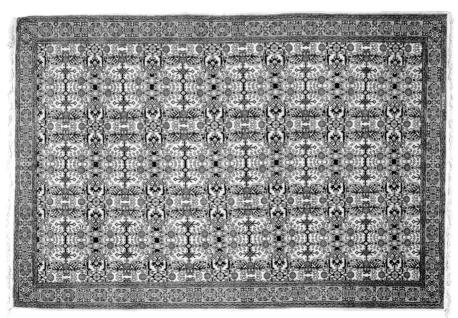

HEREKE (WOOL), 6'6" X 9'9"

more curvilinear and floral than those used in other Turkish weaving centers. Arabesques, cloudbands, vines, and tendrils are employed to fill the field, often with a central medallion. The design most characteristic of Hereke is that of a prayer rug with a mihrab which has a distinctive head-neck-and-shoulders appearance. The head portion is usually quite large, restricting the area of the field. Frequently, a small cartouche containing Arabic script is present in the upper portion of the arch. In many silk rugs the motifs are accentuated by gold threads in a weft-wrapping technique, which gives a relief effect to the pile. The inscription "Hereke" in the Western alphabet may appear in a border cartouche; recently the inscription هر ک ک ى has appeared in Arabic script.

The rugs of Hereke are finely woven and their excellent quality is reflected in their price.

EZINE Ezine is located southwest of Istanbul, about 160 miles (270 kilometers) south of the town of Canakkale on the Asiatic side of the Dardanelles. Rugs are woven in the many small surrounding villages.

Two types of designs are used in Ezine rugs. One shows a Caucasian influence and the other was adapted from the Turkish weaving center of Bergama. Caucasian-influenced rugs have designs with a large stepped medallion, capped on the top and bottom by a triangular arch, that dominates the field. These rugs also have small octagons containing multicolored stepped polygons and major serrated leaf borders as is common in many Caucasian rugs.

Ezine rugs with designs borrowed from Bergama have a field divided into two squares. The squares contain either stepped polygons within an octagon or a rectangle with arrows protruding from each side.

The background is typically red with yellow, blue, and white used for the motifs. The majority of Ezines are small, approximately 3 feet 3 inches by 4 feet 8 inches (100 by 143 centimeters).

AYVACIK The small town of Ayvacik is located approximately 17 miles (30 kilometers) southeast of Ezine.

EZINE

◆

KNOT
symmetrical

WARP
wool, light-colored

WEFT
two or more shoots,
dyed-red wool

PILE
long, shaggy wool

ENDS
very wide kelim with
decorative stripe and
plain fringe

SIDES
three cords, overcast
with wool

◆

AYVACIK

◆

KNOT
symmetrical

WARP
wool, light-colored

WEFT
two or more shoots, wool

PILE
long, shaggy wool

ENDS
wide red kelim with knotted
fringe at both ends

SIDES
three cords, overcast
with wool

◆

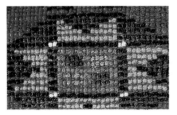

BACK OF BERGAMA

Until World War I a large portion of the population was Greek. During the population exchange after the war, most of the Greeks were resettled in Greece and Turks living in Lesbos, the Balkans, and Crete resettled in Ayvacik.

Carpets woven in both Ayvacik and Ezine usually are sold in the markets in Canakkale and often are sold under the Canakkale name. Ayvacik rugs are quite similar to those of Ezine in structure, although generally not as finely woven. The designs and motifs used in Ayvacik reflect the same Caucasian influence found in many Ezines.

One of the most common designs is a long, narrow hexagon that dominates the central field; the ends of the hexagon terminate in a pair of hooked protrusions resembling ice tongs. A column of small octagons or star-shaped motifs flanks the hexagon. The field is often a rich golden yellow color; white, red, blue, and green are used for the motifs. Ayvacik rugs are woven in small sizes.

BERGAMA, 3'6" X 5'

KNOT
symmetrical

WARP
wool, natural light-colored

WEFT
two shoots, dyed brown
or red wool

PILE
wool, medium long

ENDS
wide red kelim with
various-colored stripes

SIDES
two to four cords,
weft wrapped

◆

KOZAK
◆

KNOT
symmetrical

WARP
wool

WEFT
two or more shoots,
dyed red wool

PILE
wool, medium long

ENDS
wide kelim with striped
bands and braided fringe

SIDES
three cords,
weft wrapped

◆

BERGAMA The town of Bergama is about 30 miles (50 kilometers) east of the Aegean Sea in northwestern Turkey, on the site of the ancient Greek learning center of Pergamum. Carpets were woven here as early as the 14th century. Many carpets depicted in the 15th and 16th-century paintings of Holbein, Crivelli, and Carpaccio have been attributed to the Bergama area.

One of the most common designs used in Bergama carpets is that of a large, red diamond-shape medallion on a navy blue field. The medallion is outlined with a chain of floral motifs. At the center of the medallion is a small geometric motif from which emanate twelve rays, giving the appearance of a sun burst. Each of the four corner medallions contains a small geometric rosette.

Bergama carpets are small and tend to be squarish in shape. They generally range in size from 2 feet 8 inches by 4 feet 4 inches (80 by 130 centimeters) to 3 feet by 5 feet 6 inches (90 by 165 centimeters).

KOZAK The small town of Kozak is about 12 miles (20 kilometers) north of Bergama. Many of its inhabitants can trace their origins to the Caucasus, their ancestors having migrated to this area during the Seljuk period (11th–13th centuries). Kozak rugs resemble the rugs of the Caucasus, primarily the Kazak, with their bold geometric designs and brilliant colors. Most of the rugs woven in Kozak are sold in the markets at Bergama.

Prayer and Medallion designs are frequently used by the weavers of Kozak. Medallion carpets have either a large plain square or a square with arched protrusions at its top and bottom. Prayer-design Kozaks generally have open fields with one or two randomly placed small geometric motifs. These motifs are quite similar to those woven in Kazak and other Caucasian rugs. The main border often contains floral motifs resembling carnations. Small triangles occasionally are woven in Kozak rugs, in the kelim as well as in the pile. These triangles, called *muskas*, are symbols of good luck.

Kozaks are brilliantly colored; shades of bright red, blue, green, and white are most commonly used. Kozaks are noted for their use of the color green. They are woven in small sizes.

KOZAK, 2'6" X 5'

YAGCIBEDIR, 3'6" X 6'

BACK OF YAGCIBEDIR

YAGCIBEDIR Yagcibedir rugs are woven in Sindirgi and in the small surrounding villages 45 miles (75 kilometers) east of Bergama. Yagcibedir rugs take their name from the man who, according to legend, taught the villagers the art of carpet weaving.

Yagcibedir carpets are easily recognized by their color combinations and designs. The most common design consists of a red and white outline of a stepped hexagon superimposed on a navy blue field. A variety of small designs and motifs fill the field as well as the area inside the hexagon. The Lesghi star pattern, adopted from the Caucasian weaving center of the same name, and prayer designs are also used. White is occasionally used for the background. If an ivory-colored wool is used for the field, then red and blue are used for the motifs.

The wool used in Yagcibedir rugs is spun by hand and is of excellent quality. Occasionally the pile is sculptured, giving a bas-relief effect to the rug.

Some Yagcibedir carpets are given a heavy chemical wash to give them an aged look. Yagcibedir rugs are not always colorfast when subjected to strong light.

YAGCIBEDIR

◆

KNOT
symmetrical

WARP
natural-colored wool

WEFT
two shoots, dyed red wool

PILE
medium short

ENDS
wide red and blue
striped kelim with braided
fringe at both ends

SIDES
two wool-wrapped cords

◆

USHAK

◆

KNOT
symmetrical

WARP
wool or cotton

WEFT
two or three shoots,
wool, often dyed red,
or cotton

PILE
fine-quality wool

ENDS
small kelim with fringe
at both ends

SIDES
two cords, overcast
with wool

◆

Most Yagcibedir rugs are woven in small sizes; they range in size from small mats to 4 by 6 feet (120 by 180 centimeters). These rugs are reasonably priced.

USHAK (OUSHAK, USAK) Ushak is situated about 100 miles (160 kilometers) east of Izmir in central, western Anatolia. Weaving has been done here for at least five hundred years. Ushak carpets were some of the earliest to reach the European markets. Their bold colors and designs are depicted in Renaissance paintings by Lorenzo Lotto and Hans Holbein the Younger.

The Ushak rugs woven at the end of the 19th century were very different from the Star and Medallion Ushaks woven during the 17th and 18th centuries. The 19th-century Ushak was coarsely woven, with a thick, long pile. Because of this weave, the carpets were not very durable and consequently are often found in poor condition. Typically these Ushaks were woven with a large central medallion surrounded by an open or semifilled field, in muted and pastel shades. Because of their color combinations rugs of this era are often sought after by interior designers, and are expensive. Some of their designs are similar to those used in the Ziegler carpets from Sultanabad, and they are sometimes mislabeled as such. The 19th-century Ushaks were commonly woven in large sizes, 9 by 12 feet (275 by 365 centimeters) and larger.

During the first quarter of the 20th century, many Ushak rugs were woven in bright colors: red, blue, green, and turquoise. These rugs had a geometric central medallion and rectilinear motifs filling the field. They were woven in a variety of sizes from small mats to room-size rugs. Currently natural-dyed wool rugs with soft colors are being woven in Ushak. The designs used are copies of classic Ushak patterns.

KULA Kula is located in central western Turkey, about 81 miles (135 kilometers) east of Izmir, on the road to Ushak. Carpets were woven here as early as the 17th century. Currently weaving is done in Kula as well as the surrounding area villages.

A wide variety of designs adopted from other weaving centers as well as the centuries-old traditional designs are

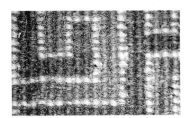

BACK OF KULA

KULA, 6' X 9'

woven. The most common designs employed by Kula weavers are the prayer rug and a medallion design. The classic Kula prayer design consists of an elongated mihrab lined with small floral motifs and a central field dominated either by a Tree-of-Life or a floral spray hanging from the apex of the mihrab. The Kula medallion design consists of a rectilinear medallion, reminiscent of old Caucasian and Turkish patterns, with a variety of small floral motifs filling the field. Many of these rugs are woven in soft colors.

Older Kula rugs were woven with wool warps and wefts, with cotton occasionally used for the wefts. Since the late 1940s the use of cotton for both warps and wefts has increased. The alternate warp threads are depressed, yielding a thicker-bodied carpet. When combined with the excellent-quality wool used for the pile, the depressed warps yield a very durable carpet. Most Kulas are woven in small sizes, although room-size rugs are sometimes found.

MELAS Melas is situated in southwest Turkey in the province of the same name. Today it is an agricultural town. It was the site of the ancient Greek town of Mylasa. Carpets have been woven here for several hundred years. Rugs are woven in Melas, in the numerous small mountain villages, and along the Aegean coast.

A prayer design indigenous to this area is composed of a

MELAS

◆

KNOT
symmetrical

WARP
natural-colored wool,
occasionally cotton

WEFT
two or more shoots,
dyed red wool in older rugs
and golden color in
newer rugs;
occasionally cotton

PILE
wool, medium to
medium long

ENDS
kelim with plain fringe
at both ends

SIDES
two to four cords, weft
wrapped or overcast
with wool

◆

diamond-shaped lozenge superimposed over the top of a prayer niche, giving a characteristic head-neck-and-shoulder appearance. The spandrel is ivory and shades of red, brown, yellow, and ivory are used for the stylized motifs. In older carpets the prayer niche is dull brick red; in newer carpets, it is either reddish brown or brown.

Ada Melas (commonly called "Melas stripe" or "Melas column") carpets are woven in the village of Karaova. The central field of these carpets is disproportionately small, being restricted by an unusually wide major border made up of reciprocal salients, quite similar and often identical to each other. The central field design is often echoed in the border. The colors of Ada Melas are more muted than those of other types of Melas rugs.

The medallion design is woven in the village of Karjese. A large central medallion is placed within a comparatively small field. This type of Melas is not as common as the prayer design or the Ada Melas.

Melas carpets are coarsely woven on a woolen foundation. The pile is medium to medium long. Small sizes of 3 by 6 feet (90 by 180 centimeters) and runners approximately 2 feet 6 inches by 10 feet (80 by 305 centimeters) are most common. The colors woven currently in Melas carpets are light beige, light brown, yellow, and light green. In older carpets, brick red is often used for the field.

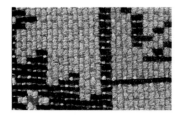

BACK OF MELAS

MELAS, 3'6" X 7'

DOSEMEALTI, 3'6" X 6'

DOSEMEALTI

◆

KNOT
symmetrical

WARP
natural-colored wool

WEFT
two or more shoots, dark-
colored wool

PILE
wool, medium in length

ENDS
kelim with braided fringe at
one end, looped at the other

SIDES
two cords, overcast
with wool

◆

KONYA

◆

KNOT
symmetrical

WARP
wool

WEFT
two or more shoots,
dyed red wool

PILE
wool, medium in length

ENDS
wide striped kelim with
braided fringe at both ends

SIDES
two to four cords, weft
wrapped with foundation
weft or added wefts

◆

DOSEMEALTI Dosemealti is a small town five miles (8 kilometers) north of the Mediterranean Sea and the city of Antalya in southern Turkey. Carpets are woven in Dosemealti and the surrounding area.

Carpet weaving in Dosemealti is primarily a cottage industry. Women do the weaving as well as spinning most of their own wool. The wool used is from the local sheep, pastured in the plateaus around Antalya, and is an excellent quality. The dyes used are natural. Red and blue are the predominant colors, with white, yellow, and green used in the motifs. A hexagonal medallion on a field filled with small geometric motifs is the design most frequently used. Dosemealti carpets are usually small mats to 3 feet 6 inches by 6 feet (105 by 180 centimeters). Runners are also woven.

KONYA The ancient city of Konya was known as Kuwanna by the Hittites four thousand years ago and as Iconium by the Romans. It was the capital of the Seljuk sultanate of Rum. Konya is located in the heart of the Anatolian Plateau in south-central Turkey, approximately 150 miles (250 kilometers) south of Ankara, the capital.

The Konya weaving district is one of Turkey's largest and most important rug-producing areas. It consists of the city of Konya and the villages of Ladik, Karaman, Karapinar, Kecemuslu, Innice, Obruk, and Eregli.

BACK OF KONYA

KONYA, 4' X 6'

LADIK

◆

KNOT
symmetrical

WARP
wool

WEFT
two or more shoots, wool

PILE
wool, short

ENDS
kelim with braided
fringe at both ends

SIDES
two cords, weft wrapped
with wool

◆

Konya is noted for its weaving of prayer rugs with a prayer arch surmounted on a pair of columns on a red field. A lamp or floral motif is often suspended from the mihrab. Gold, green, and ivory are used for the motifs. Other designs used are the Medallion design and a repeated Memling Gul pattern. Red and gold are the predominant colors. Most Konya rugs are woven in small sizes.

LADIK The village of Ladik, located 21 miles (35 kilometers) northwest of Konya, is one of the most important Konya-area villages. Ladik is known for the weaving of prayer rugs with a tulip motif panel. The field of these rugs can be divided into three parts: mihrab and lower field, spandrels, and a wide panel containing tulip motifs. The tulips have long stalks and may number three, five, or seven. The tulip panel may appear either above the spandrels, below the field, or in rare occasions two panels are used. The field is most frequently red, although ivory and blue are used. A hanging lamp, stalk with flowers, or floral motif may be suspended from the prayer arch.

LADIK, 3'6" X 7'

The spandrels usually contain stylized flowers or a water ewer on each side. The main border is usually composed of the stylized Lily and Rosette border design. Ladik rugs are usually woven in an elongated format, 3 feet 6 inches by 6 feet 6 inches (110 by 200 centimeters).

KONYA-LADIK The term "Konya-Ladik" is used to refer to rugs currently being woven in Ladik. Modern Ladiks are different from those woven in Ladik prior to World War I. Konya-Ladiks are woven with cotton warp and weft threads and excellent-quality wool pile. The most common designs used are floral and medallion patterns adopted from Persian weaving centers such as Tabriz.

DEMIRCI The town of Demirci is approximately 25 miles (40 kilometers) south of the city of Bursa in northwestern Turkey. Demirci rugs are referred to in some Oriental rug books as "Komurdju Kulas." The rugs woven here are reminiscent of Transylvanian carpets of the 16th and 17th centuries. Most production of hand-knotted carpets had stopped by the 1930s.

The most common design used in Demirci carpets is that of a large shield-type hexagonal medallion, which gives the impression of a double prayer niche. The medallion is superimposed on a dark-brown or black field, with shades of light blue, green, ivory, and yellow used for the stylized motifs.

KONYA-LADIK

◆

KNOT
symmetrical

WARP
cotton

WEFT
two shoots, cotton

PILE
wool, medium thick

ENDS
kelim with fringe

SIDES
overcast with wool

◆

DEMIRCI, 4' x 5'

DEMIRCI

◆

KNOT
symmetrical

WARP
natural-colored wool

WEFT
two or more shoots,
dyed-red wool

PILE
wool

ENDS
striped kelim with plain
fringe at both ends

SIDES
two cords, wrapped
red wool

◆

KAYSERI

◆

KNOT
symmetrical

WARP
cotton

WEFT
two shoots, cotton

PILE
wool, artificial silk, or silk

ENDS
small kelim with
plain fringe

SIDES
two cords, wrapped
with cotton

◆

A lamp is often suspended from the niches and the field is outlined by stylized carnations. The wide main border is composed of a meandering vine with stylized floral motifs and carnations. Rugs woven at the beginning of the 20th century often were made with synthetic-dyed wool which faded when exposed to sunlight. Demirci rugs tend to be small and squarish in shape, approximately 4 by 5 feet (120 by 150 centimeters).

KAYSERI Kayseri lies in the heart of the Anatolian plateau at the foot of Mount Erciyas. Known as Caesarea under Roman rule, Kayseri was the capital of the province of Cappadocia. Major east-west trade routes have passed through Kayseri for hundreds of years and it is still a market center for rugs from the surrounding area.

The designs woven in Kayseri carpets tend to be more curvilinear and floral than those of other Turkish weaving centers. Structurally Kayseri carpets can be divided into three types according to the material used for the pile: silk, artificial silk, or wool.

Silk rugs are woven with excellent-quality Bursa silk for the pile as well as for the warp and weft threads. They are often woven with metallic threads to accentuate certain designs and motifs.

Artificial silk (ipekli) pile rugs are also known as "Kayseri floss," "art silk," "Kayseri silk," "Turkish silk," or "mercerized cotton." The material used for the pile is usually a combination of waste silk blended with rayon and mercerized cotton. Having a silky luster and feel, to the untrained eye they resemble silk rugs. Designs woven in these rugs are adopted from Persian weaving centers as well as from 19th-century Ghiordes and Konya Turkish rugs. The *saff*, a unique design with multiple mihrabs side by side, is also commonly woven. The artificial silk rugs do not withstand wear very well. These rugs are often sold by unscrupulous rug merchants as pure silk rugs. Tour books even caution the unsuspecting traveler about the notorious Kayseri carpets.

One of the easiest ways to tell the difference between mercerized cotton and silk is to wet a small portion of the rug. Mercerized cotton will feel like cotton; silk will maintain its silky feel.

The third type of Kayseri is woven with *wool* pile. The wool used is an excellent quality and is trimmed quite short. The designs commonly used are adopted from the Persian rugs of Tabriz and Isfahan as well as Turkish weaving centers.

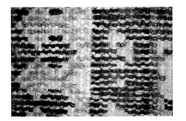

BACK OF KAYSERI

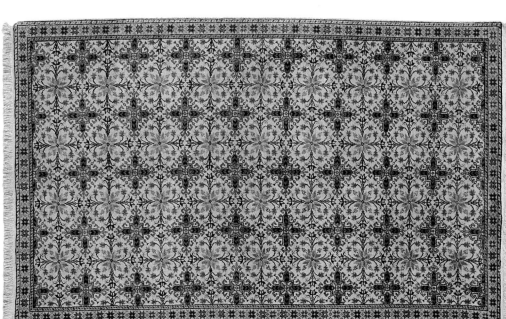

KAYSERI, 6'6" X 9'9"

Kayseri carpets are woven in small sizes up to 6 feet 6 inches by 9 feet 9 inches (2 by 3 meters); silk and artificial silk carpets are generally woven in small sizes.

KIRSHEHIR Kirshehir lies in the heart of central Turkey halfway between Ankara and Kayseri. The rugs of Kirshehir are brightly colored with combinations of cherry red, yellow, and turquoise. Red is commonly used for the field portion in Prayer and Medallion carpets. The rugs are finely woven with soft, lustrous wool.

The most common designs woven in Kirshehir are the Prayer, Medallion, and *mazarlik*. In the Medallion and Prayer design carpets, the field often is restricted at the top and bottom by a panel decorated with floral motifs. The *mazarlik* (cemetery) design is composed of a prayer niche with stylized willow trees and mausoleums on a dark-colored field. Rugs of this type are used in funerals in Anatolia. They are woven as a family effort and usually are passed down from generation to generation.

The rugs of Kirshehir are woven generally in small sizes, approximately 3 feet 5 inches by 5 feet (104 by 150 centimeters). Runners are also woven.

MUDJAR The small village of Mudjar is located 20 miles (32 kilometers) southeast of Kirshehir. It is noted for its weaving of prayer rugs with a stepped mihrab, surmounted by an arrow.

KIRSHEHIR, 4' X 6'

KIRSHEHIR

◆

KNOT
symmetrical

WARP
light-colored wool

WEFT
two or more shoots,
red wool

PILE
wool

ENDS
red kelim with plain
fringe at both ends

SIDES
two cords, wrapped
with wool

◆

MUDJAR, 3'9" X 6'

MUDJAR

◆

KNOT
symmetrical

WARP
wool, occasionally cotton
in recent rugs

WEFT
two shoots, wool dyed
red or brown

PILE
wool, medium in length

ENDS
red kelim with plain fringe
at both ends

SIDES
two to four cords,
weft wrapped

◆

The field may be either open or contain a hanging lamp or another type of motif suspended from the arch. The field and the sides of the prayer niche may be lined with a series of Greek key motifs or stylized carnations. The field is almost always red with a gold, yellow, or green in the main border or spandrel. The main border is wide and contains a repeated rosettelike motif. The colors used are rich, saturated tones. Mudjar rugs are woven primarily in small sizes.

KARS The city of Kars was founded in the 8th century by Armenians. It was captured by the Seljuks in the 11th century and by the Ottomans in 1514. Kars is located in the northeast corner of Turkey, 45 miles (75 kilometers) from the border of Armenia. Traditionally the Kars area had a large Armenian population; only a small Armenian population remains in the area today.

KNOT
symmetrical

WARP
wool; cotton in recent rugs

WEFT
two or more shoots, wool;
cotton in recent rugs

PILE
wool, loosely knotted

ENDS
wide kelim with plain
fringe at both ends

SIDES
two or more cords,
weft overcast

◆

KARS, 4' x 6'

Rugs known as Kars are woven in Kars and the surrounding area. Most of the designs used are adopted from the Caucasian weaving centers of Kazak, Karabagh, and Kuba. The name "Kars Kazaks" is sometimes given to these rugs. Designs tend to be large-scale, with one or more medallions of various shapes occupying the center field. The colors of Kars rugs often appear muddy when compared to the clear, saturated shades of Kazak rugs. The wool used in Kars rugs is coarse and not as lustrous as that used in Kazaks.

Some Kars rugs are given a heavy wash to give them an aged or old appearance. In some rugs the black and dark-brown wool has been trimmed to give the impression of corrosion, which comes with age in natural-dyed brown and black wool. The majority of rugs are woven in small sizes up to 5 by 8 feet (180 by 245 centimeters).

DOBAG DOBAG is an acronym for Dogal Boya Arastirma ve Gelistirme Projesi. This project was begun in Turkey in 1981 to reintroduce the use of natural dyes, hand-spun wool, and traditional carpet designs.

The project began in the mountain villages around the towns of Ayvacik and Yuntdag, in western Turkey. Women do the carding, spinning, and weaving in their homes. The wool used is of an excellent quality and withstands wear quite well. They also dye their own wool, with natural dye sources.

Designs used are geometric and based on local tradition. The weaver is given a freedom of expression in the designs woven and is encouraged to use her imagination. Repeated geometric motifs, central medallion, or several geometric medallions are commonly used patterns.

DOBAG rugs are not chemically washed to tone down their colors or artificially aged by chemicals, burning, or cutting. They will obtain a natural patina through daily use.

The DOBAG rugs are sold through co-ops and exported directly to authorized dealers throughout the world. They are woven in a variety of sizes from small mats to 5 by 7 feet (150 by 210 centimeters). Runners are also woven.

DOBAG, 4' X 6'

PEKING, 4' X 6'5"

nine

RUGS OF CHINA AND EASTERN TURKESTAN

he origins of Chinese carpet weaving are unclear. It is generally believed that hand-knotted carpets first appeared in Gansu and Ningxia with the eastward wanderings of nomads from Xinjiang and Central Asia. Fragments of knotted carpets from the 3rd century B.C. have been found at Lou Lan and Niya in Xinjiang. Weaving was almost exclusively done in northwest China until the last quarter of the 19th century, with the exception of the court carpets woven in Peking (Beijing) as early as the 1700s. These early carpets were utilitarian, used as bedding and *k'ang* covers. The k'ang, comparable to a couch, was used by the Chinese as protection from the cold. In Buddhist monasteries, rugs were used for pillar covers, seat and back covers, door curtains, and prayer mats. In addition, hand-knotted carpets were used as saddle blankets, interior lining of yurt walls, and floor coverings.

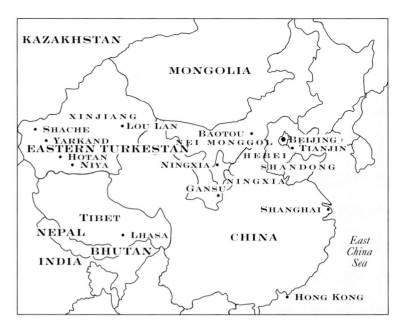

CHINA AND EASTERN TURKESTAN

CHINESE RUGS

The greatest developments in Chinese carpet weaving came under the patronage of the Emperor Ch'ien Lung in the second half of the 18th century. In the 1870s the Emperor T'ung Chih established a technical school for weaving in Peking. A Buddhist monk from Gansu was brought to the workshop to teach the art of carpet weaving. Foreign interest in Chinese carpets began in the late 19th century. By the early 20th century the demand for Chinese carpets was so great that weaving factories were quickly established. Peking (Beijing) and Tientsin (Tianjin) became the primary manufacturing centers for rugs woven largely for export. Designs were and still are influenced by foreign tastes and market demands.

Currently the carpet-weaving industry in China is directed by the Carpet Branch of the China National Native Produce and Animal By-Products Import and Export Corporation. The major carpet-weaving branches are located in Beijing, Shanghai, Hebei, Shandong, Dalien, Tianjin, and Xinjiang. Each branch has its own specialized area of rug production, with numerous factories within each branch. Beijing, Tianjin, and Shanghai produce the greatest volume of carpets for export.

Structure. Modern Chinese carpets are similar in construction to their predecessors. The asymmetrical knot is used. Wool, cotton, and silk are the most important raw materials used in the weaving. The majority of rugs are woven with wool pile and cotton warp and weft threads. Silk pile rugs are woven with either cotton or silk warp threads and cotton wefts. Other fibers, such as goat hair, yak hair, flax, and jute, are used in inexpensive carpets.

Both imported and local wool are used in Chinese carpets. The Chinese wool comes from the western provinces; it is of excellent quality and is lustrous and soft to the touch. The silky luster of the pile is from a chemical wash given the carpets before export. The silk used is from the provinces of Zhejing, Jiangsu, and Hebei.

Quality of the modern Chinese carpet is determined by a series of structural variables. These include line, yarn ply, height of pile, spun wool, and type of weave used.

Tightness of weave is determined by the number of warp threads used in a given measure. In China this is defined as *line*, a term that refers to the number of pairs of warp threads, or knots per linear foot. A 90-line rug has 90 knots per linear foot, which is equivalent to 56 knots per square inch. The quality in wool rugs is 70, 80, 90, 100, 120, 240, 260, 300, and even higher. However, orders can be placed for any specified knot count.

The wool used for the pile is spun either by machine or by hand. (The majority of rugs are woven with machine-spun wool, which is more evenly spun and uniform in appearance.) The wool is either four- or five-ply. Four-ply yarn is generally used for most line qualities; five-ply is used in the 90-line quality.

The length of the pile varies depending on the line and design woven: $\frac{2}{8}$, $\frac{3}{8}$, $\frac{4}{8}$, or $\frac{5}{8}$ inch. In general the higher the line count, the shorter the pile is trimmed, thus ensuring a crisper design. Very finely knotted Persian-design rugs are woven with $\frac{2}{8}$-inch pile. The majority of silk rugs are also woven with $\frac{2}{8}$-inch pile.

The appearance of the back of the rug is another structural

variable: open back or closed back. Open-back rugs have wefts that are clearly visible from the back. In closed-back rugs the wefts are not visible from the back since the knots completely cover the wefts. Because of the warp depression and the manner in which the knots are tied, more wool is used in the weaving of closed-back rugs. Approximately 20 percent more wool is used in a 90-line closed-back than in the same size 90-line rug with an open back.

Many Chinese rugs have pile that is embossed or sculptured. The motif to be embossed or sculptured is woven with slightly longer pile than the rest of the carpet. After the carpet has been completed, the raised areas are accentuated by trimming parts of the motif. This is done on a slant to give a relief or sculptured effect to the pile.

Design. Designs woven in Chinese rugs are simple, well-composed patterns. They are not nearly as elaborate and crowded with small motifs as are designs from some Persian weaving centers. Chinese designs are crisp and the overall patterns are well proportioned. Traditionally many of the designs used in Chinese carpets are inspired by religious beliefs and cultural traditions.

Weaving Centers. Carpet weaving remained almost exclusively in the northwest provinces of Gansu, Baotou, and Ningxia until the last of the 19th century. The weavers had their own styles, designs, and color combinations. They retained these distinctive characteristics for centuries, resisting the foreign influences that affected the commercial centers of Beijing and Tianjin.

GANSU (KANSU) For centuries Gansu has been a marketplace, strategically placed at the juncture of the northern and southern trade routes from the West to Beijing.

Gansu rugs are woven with cotton warp and weft threads. The pile is a soft wool which is loosely knotted. The majority of Gansu rugs are woven approximately 2 by 4 feet (60 by 120 centimeters) in size, which makes them easily portable and adaptable for a number of purposes.

The rugs of Gansu are predominantly blue and white, with the designs and motifs in three shades of blue. The two most

GANSU

◆

KNOT
asymmetrical

WARP
cotton

WEFT
two shoots,
undyed cotton

PILE
soft wool, loosely knotted

ENDS
knotted fringe at
both ends

SIDES
single cord,
weft wrapped

◆

GANSU SADDLE BLANKET, 2' X 5'

BAOTOU

◆

KNOT
asymmetrical

WARP
cotton

WEFT
two shoots, cotton

PILE
soft wool, loosely knotted

ENDS
knotted fringe
at both ends

SIDES
single cord,
weft wrapped

◆

BAOTOU, 3' X 5'5"

common designs are the medallion design and a scenic representation containing a stag or a horse standing under a fir tree with a crane. The medallion design consists of a central floral motif, often peonies, with a stepped-fret motif in each corner.

Since the 1970s Gansu has been a center for weaving carpets with an "antique finish." These carpets are given a chemical wash to give an old appearance to the rug. This wash often imparts a brownish cast to the wool. A heavy "antique" wash leaves the wool rather dry and drab. Some Gansu rugs are woven with vegetable-dyed wool.

BAOTOU (PAOTOU) "Baotou" is a collective term applied to carpets that were woven throughout the province of Suiyuan, now part of Inner Mongolia. These rugs were collected for market in the capital and largest city of Baotou.

Baotou rugs are similar to those of Gansu in structure as well as in designs employed. Like the rugs from the northwest provinces, the wool used in Baotou rugs is soft and loosely knotted and is not suitable for heavy traffic areas.

The designs used in old Baotou rugs are large in relation to the size of the rug, and in many instances no border is used. The most common designs are vases of flowers, animals, and large naturalistic landscapes featuring animals. The scenic-design rugs are often woven in a format wider than long, approximately 4 feet 3 inches by 6 feet 6 inches (130 by 200 centimeters).

NINGXIA

◆

KNOT
asymmetrical

WARP
cotton

WEFT
two shoots, undyed cotton

PILE
soft, silky wool

ENDS
knotted fringe at both ends

SIDES
single or double cord,
overcast with cotton

◆

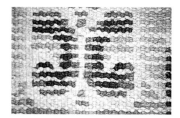

BACK OF NINGXIA

During the 1970s Baotou, like Gansu, became a center for the weaving of "antique finish" carpets. These rugs are woven with old Beijing-type designs and then chemically washed to give the carpet an aged appearance. Rugs of this type are woven in the 90-line quality in sizes of 6 by 9 feet (182 by 275 centimeters) and larger.

NINGXIA (NINGSHIA) The town of Ningxia is located near the Great Wall of China in the northern frontier province of Ningxia. Ningxia, like Bukhara and Samarkand, was a marketplace for rugs woven in the surrounding area.

Ningxia rugs are woven with a soft, fleecy wool pile that is rather loosely knotted. The pile of some rugs has been "carved" to accentuate certain designs and motifs. Ningxia carpets are known for their combination of beautiful colors and the numerous shades of color employed. The background color is most commonly beige, camel, or yellow; the motifs are in shades of blue; and red is used as a minor accent.

A wide variety of designs were woven throughout Ningxia. The medallion design was one of the most commonly used. Naturalistic depictions of a horse and a stag were also woven. In recent years, Ningxia has become a center for the weaving of rugs with natural dyes, in Beijing-type designs.

NINGXIA, 3' X 6'

PEKING

◆

KNOT
asymmetrical

WARP
thin cotton

WEFT
two shoots, cotton

PILE
wool, medium

ENDS
plain fringe at both ends

SIDES
single cord,
weft wrapped

◆

TIENTSIN, 4' X 6'

PEKING   Early Peking* rugs resembled the rugs from the northwest provinces in design and color combination. A central medallion was placed in a field, with several symbolic motifs, surrounded by several borders. The palette generally was limited to three shades of blue, gold, buff, and ivory. The *shou* (Chinese character symbolizing long life), floral, bat, and dragon motifs in a rounded shape were used for the central medallion. Several Buddhist, Taoist, or Confucian symbols were placed in the field. The main border often contained the peony design, and the running-T pattern frequently was found in the minor borders.

After the fall of the Ch'ing dynasty, the five-clawed dragon became a popular design for rugs woven in Peking. Before that time the use of the five-clawed, or imperial, dragon had been forbidden for use except for the emperor.

Peking rugs are supple and rather floppy. They have a lustrous and soft wool pile. Weft threads are clearly visible on the back of the rug. The majority of Peking rugs were woven in large sizes, 8 by 10 feet (245 by 305 centimeters) and 9 by 12 feet (275 by 365 centimeters).

TIENTSIN   Tientsin** rapidly developed as a weaving center for the North American and European markets. The designs and colors used in these rugs were dictated by these markets. During the 1920s, many Tientsin rugs were sparsely decorated. The entire pattern may consist of only two floral bouquets in diagonal corners, with no border arrangement. Pictorial carpets with a design of a temple, pagoda, junk (Chinese ship), camelback bridge, or vase were used.

During the 1930s tone-on-tone rugs (Self-Tone Embossed) were introduced with designs that were incised and carved into the pile. Art Deco and Aubusson (Esthetic) designs were also developed during this period. Other rugs may contain a combination of motifs, such as a pagoda, vase, or junk. In some instances a branch of flowers would not be contained solely

*Although the name Beijing is used in the Pinyin system, these rugs are still referred to in the Oriental rug trade as Peking.
**Although the name Tianjin is used in Pinyin, these rugs are still known in the Oriental rug trade as Tientsin.

TIENTSIN

◆

KNOT
asymmetrical

WARP
thick cotton

WEFT
two shoots, cotton

PILE
thick, dense wool

ENDS
wide kelim with knotted
fringe at both ends

SIDES
single cord, overcast
with wool

◆

within the field but would also extend into the border. Color combinations used were different: purple with green, mauve with dark blue, caramel with green, purple with gold.

Tientsin rugs have a thicker, denser pile than Peking rugs. Thick cotton was used for the warps. The closed-back technique was developed in Tientsin. Tienstin rugs were woven in a wide variety of sizes and shapes: oval, round, semicircular, and the standard rectangular shapes.

MODERN RUGS Recently the Chinese have organized and redefined the standard design groups used since the Chinese Revolution. The designs are now divided into Standard Chinese, Esthetic, Xinkiang, Antique Finish, Tapestry, and Persian groups.

Standard Chinese. Standard Chinese designs include floral and medallion patterns. These designs are well proportioned and are sparsely decorated with a central medallion on a large expanse of open field. Several floral or Chinese motifs are placed in the field. These designs are inspired by religious beliefs and cultural traditions. A *shou*, bat, dragon, or floral medallion on an open field or a field with several Chinese motifs is surrounded by a relatively simple border pattern.

Esthetic. The Esthetic design was developed in the 1920s in Tientsin by foreign merchants for the export market. The

STANDARD CHINESE
DESIGN, 5' X 8'

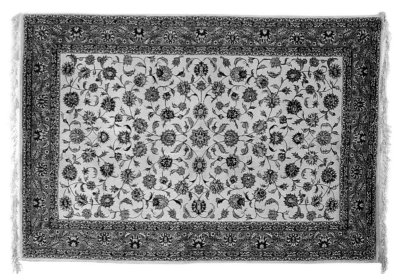

PERSIAN DESIGN, 6' X 9'

design is inspired by French Aubusson rugs. Esthetic design consists of a central medallion containing a large floral bouquet surrounded by a scalloped floral border. The field of the rug either is open or may contain several floral sprays. The pile is carved, further accentuating the designs and motifs.

Xinjiang. Rugs of this design are woven in Xinjiang. Designs are based on traditional Khotan, Kashgar, and Yarkand designs from Eastern Turkestan. The *ay gul* medallion, pomegranate tree, lattice pattern, and *saffs* are most frequently used. Traditional tones of red, orange, pink, blue, ocher, and brown are also used. Xinjiang rugs are woven in the 90-, 110-, and 120-line quality with ⅜-inch pile.

Antique Finish rugs have designs adopted from the older rugs from the northwest provinces. Antique Finish rugs are woven in the three shades of blue with ivory and a light tan or brown. They are woven in Inner Mongolia and northern China in 100-line quality with ⅜-inch pile, similar to the Peking rugs of the early 20th century. These carpets are given an antique wash to give them an aged appearance.

Tapestry rugs are pictorial. They are woven in a huge variety of patterns: Chinese landscapes, the Great Wall, birds, animals, and scenes from Chinese history and mythology are portrayed. These rugs are woven in both silk and wool pile and usually in small sizes. Some of the best weavers are employed in making this type of design. Tapestry rugs are woven in a wide range of 110- to 120-line quality with ⅜-inch pile to 200-line or more with ⅖-inch pile.

Persian design rugs have been developed to fill the void in Persian rugs on the American market since the U.S. embargo on rugs from Iran in the 1980s. Beautifully executed copies of Isfahan, Nain, Kashan, and Kerman rugs are woven with central Medallion, Shah Abbas, and Tree-of-Life patterns in colors similar to those from Persian weaving centers. Traditional red and blue backgrounds are used as well as pastel shades.

Persian-design rugs are woven with wool pile, silk pile, and a combination of wool with silk highlights. The height of the pile varies, ⅖ or ⅜ inch, depending on the line count. The higher the line count, the shorter the pile is trimmed, rendering the intricate patterns crisper and clearer.

XINJIANG, 6' X 9'

KHOTAN, 5' X 9'

EASTERN TURKESTAN

Eastern Turkestan is located in Xinjiang (Sinkiang), an Autonomous Region within the People's Republic of China. The oasis towns of Hotan (Khotan), Yarkand, and Shache (Kashgar) were the primary sources of carpets woven in this region. Until recently, the population was of Turkic stock, spoke a Turkic language, and was Muslim.

Rugs from Eastern Turkestan were often referred to in the West as "Samarkands" and in China as "Gansus." Samarkand, in Uzbekistan, was for centuries the major marketplace for the rugs from this area, which were destined for Western markets. Gansu also was a marketplace, the entry point for rugs of Eastern Turkestan entering China.

Even though the Silk Route and other caravan routes crossed Eastern Turkestan, Western influences on the carpets of this area were relatively few until the last half of the 19th century. Designs of these rugs show a blending of Chinese, Turkoman, and Caucasian influences.

The weave in older Xinjiang carpets is rather coarse, ranging from approximately 40 to 100 knots per square inch. The wool is soft and not very durable; consequently, many of the carpets did not withstand wear very well. The rugs of Xinjiang are usually asymmetrically knotted with two-ply woolen yarn to create a thicker pile; symmetrical knots were used in older rugs.

Silk pile carpets were woven in Eastern Turkestan, many

KNOT
asymmetrical;
symmetrical in older rugs

WARP
cotton; wool in older rugs

WEFT
two or more shoots; cotton
or, in older rugs, wool

PILE
two-ply soft wool

ENDS
narrow kelim, with plain
fringe at one end and looped
fringe at the other

SIDES
single cord,
overcast with wool

◆

of which have been attributed to the Kashgar oasis. These rugs were woven with either silk or cotton used for the warp and weft threads. Other carpets were woven with silk pile which was interwoven with a highlighting of metal threads. These threads were made by winding thin strips of silver or gold-plated copper around a silk or cotton core, and were then woven into the carpet in a soumak stitch to give a relief effect. Carpets with metallic thread were woven in Persian-style patterns.

The medallion design was one of the most common designs woven in the Khotan oasis. This design consists of a central medallion, resembling a flattened disc, called an *ay gul* (moon motif). The central medallion may also appear flanked by two medallions of similar type or may have only two medallions. The medallions may contain pomegranate or cloud motifs, floral figures, or a degenerated gul motif. Red and golden yellow were the most common ground colors used; the medallion was either blue or yellow.

The pomegranate-vase pattern is one of the oldest and most frequently used designs in rugs from Eastern Turkestan. The design consists of a pomegranate tree bearing fruit; the tree emanates from a vase situated at the base of the field. The field may be either blue or golden yellow, with rose-red tree and fruit motifs or, less often, a burnt orange field with a blue tree and fruits. The major border often consists of a wave-and-cloud border. Typically, these rugs are slightly more than twice as long as they are wide.

Other designs employed in the Khotan oasis are the cloud-lattice pattern and the *saff*. The cloud-lattice pattern is composed of interconnecting cloudbands that form a network throughout the field of the carpet. The *saff* is composed of multiple prayer mihrabs placed side by side.

The new rugs from Xinkiang are more finely woven with a thicker and heavier, more durable pile than their earlier counterparts (see page 159). They are woven either in the 90- or 110-line quality. The warp and weft threads are of cotton. New Xinkiang carpets are woven with a pleasing combination of different shades of blue, brown, cream, and rose red. The majority of rugs are woven in small sizes up to 5 by 9 feet (152 by 275 centimeters).

NEPAL, 4' x 7'

ten

RUGS OF TIBET AND NEPAL

ibet is a vast area in the heart of Central Asia. It is bordered on three sides by the world's highest mountain ranges: on the north by the Kunlun and Nanshan mountain ranges, on the west by the Karakoram and Ladakh ranges, and on the south by the Himalayas. When Britain and Russia expanded their empires into Central Asia, Tibetans became frightened for their way of life and religion and closed their borders to all foreigners except the Chinese. This forbidden land remained closed to Western visitors until 1904. For 350 years Tibet was a religious kingdom ruled by a Dalai Lama. In 1965 it became an Autonomous Region in the People's Republic of China.

Tibet traditionally was an agricultural society with farming and herding as the most important source of individual income. Raw wool made up a large portion of its export. Carpet

RUG-WEAVING AREAS OF TIBET AND NEPAL

TIBET

◆

KNOT
Tibetan knotting technique,
asymmetrical knot

WARP
cotton; wool in older rugs

WEFT
two shoots, cotton;
wool in older rugs

PILE
thick, heavy wool, with a
ridged appearance

ENDS
kelim with looped fringe
at one end and plain fringe at
the other, red cloth binding,
or long shaggy fringe

SIDES
single cord, overcast with
wool, or red cloth binding or
long shaggy fringe

◆

weaving was done primarily in the monastery towns and urban centers of Shigatse, Gyantse, Lhasa, Sakaya, Kyirong, and Khampa Dzong. The greatest concentration of weaving was done in and around the cities of Gyantse, Shigatse, and Lhasa. Weaving was also done by individuals in their homes and by nomads.

TIBET (XIZANG)

Tibetan carpets are utilitarian. Small rugs were made for horse blankets, saddle rugs, and mats for sitting and sleeping. Mats for sitting and backrests for seats were woven in 3-foot (90-centimeter) squares. Sleeping mats approximately 3 feet by 5 feet 6 inches (90 by 170 centimeters) were used by Tibetans in their homes as well as by nomads. Saddle rugs were usually made in pairs, one to put under the saddle and the other to cover the top of the saddle.

Larger rugs were made for floor covering as well as for other purposes. In monasteries, rugs were used for door curtains, temple aisle runners, and pillar rugs. Temple aisle runners were woven up to 33 feet (10 meters) in length. These were divided by design into 3-foot (90-centimeter) square sections for monks to sit on in rows. The pillar carpets were

TIBETAN, 2' x 3'6"

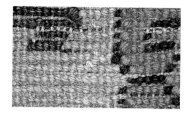

BACK OF TIBETAN RUG

woven in one-directional designs, often with a dragon. Many pillar rugs were woven in such a way that the figure of the dragon wrapped around the pillar, in a continuous coil of the dragon and its tail.

Antique Tibetan carpets are coarsely woven on a woolen foundation. Wool was used solely for the warp and weft threads until after World War I, when the use of cotton for the weft threads was first introduced.

The Tibetan use of a metal or wooden rod in knotting carpets is unique. Instead of cutting the yarn after each individual knot, the yarn is looped around consecutive pairs of warp threads and then around the rod (see page 168). After the row has been completed, a knife is run along the rod, cutting the pile. This gives the pile a ridged appearance.

Older Tibetan carpets often are bordered on all four sides with red cloth or felt. Some Tibetan rugs are surrounded by a long, thick, shaggy fringe.

The designs and motifs used in Tibetan rugs often combine Taoist symbols, Buddhist ritual objects, and Chinese-style medallions. The designs can be grouped by the field composition into medallion, floral, animal, lattice, and repeated geometric designs.

TIBETAN, 6' X 9'

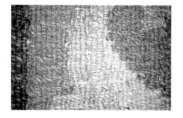

BACK OF TIBETAN RUG

Medallion-design carpets may have either a central medallion or three medallions. The medallion may appear as a Chinese-style floral medallion or simply a ritualistic object such as a double *dorge* (a small object used by Buddhists in meditation). The medallion may be placed in a field which is empty, or semifilled with floral motifs, cloudbands, or Buddhist ritual objects, or filled with a repeated geometric pattern.

Floral-design rugs are composed of large floral blossoms or repeated floral designs. Stylized lotus, peonies, and chrysanthemum patterns are used.

Tigers, symbols of power in Tibetan culture, were depicted in Tibetan rugs. Depictions of flayed tiger skins were used in monasteries for ritualistic purposes. A tiger motif may appear as a single tiger skin, a double-headed skin, two confronting tiger skins, or an abstract depiction with only the tiger stripes. Also pictured in Tibetan rugs are the dragon, phoenix, crane, bat, and snow lion. Human figures, skulls, and skeletons are also occasionally depicted.

Lattice-design carpets have a field divided into small diamond-shaped compartments. The compartments are filled with small multicolored geometric or floral motifs.

Repeated-geometric patterns used a checkerboard, diaper, or frog-foot pattern to fill the field. The small, repeated patterns were used alone or often in combination with a central medallion.

Tibetan border designs include a meandering flower and vine pattern, running-T, cloud-mountain-wave pattern, pearl, and swastika patterns. Some Tibetan rugs have no borders.

Currently carpets are woven in Tibet by both men and women in both government and privately owned factories, as well as by individuals in their homes. These modern Tibetan rugs are more finely woven than their earlier counterparts. Many rugs are made with a thick pile in either soft pastel colors or with natural undyed wool. Since most rugs are for commercial production, they are produced in standard colors, sizes, and designs. Many of the designs used in modern Tibetan rugs are simple: there may be an open field with no design surrounded by a single border or several borders, or an open field with stepped-fret motifs in each corner surrounded by a border arrangement, or a central medallion surrounded by a border. Traditional designs and color combinations still are woven in floral patterns and Chinese-style medallions.

Tibetan rugs come in standard sizes ranging from 3 by 6 feet (90 by 182 centimeters) to 9 by 12 feet (274 by 365 centimeters). Larger rugs up to 10 by 14 feet (305 by 426 centimeters) and runners are also produced.

"Tibetan" carpets are woven in Nepal and northern India. The total output of new carpets from Tibet is small when compared with Tibetan carpets from Nepal.

The Kingdom of Nepal is a small country squeezed between India and the Xizang Autonomous Region of China (Tibet). Nepal and northern India became home to 80,000 Tibetans who left their homeland in 1959–60. Centers were set up for these refugees, many of whom were experienced weavers, and in the 1960s carpet-weaving workshops were established in many of the refugee centers. SATA, the Swiss Association for Technical Assistance, helped establish weaving workshops at the Jawalakhel Handicraft Center with the purpose of expanding the carpet market in Europe. Carpets produced in these workshops are typically Tibetan in character and are sold as "Tibetan" carpets.

Before the development of carpet potential for Nepal, weaving was limited to mats and small rugs with traditional Tibetan designs. Many of these rugs were woven by individuals or in small workshops. Since 1970, carpet weaving has expanded from a small industry to the largest employer in the country. Exports have risen from 200,000 to over 2 million square meters. Currently the largest portion of the weaving population is non-Tibetan.

The majority of rugs woven in Nepal are commercially produced in standardized patterns, sizes, and color combi-

NEPAL

KNOT
asymmetrical and Tibetan
knotting technique

WARP
cotton, occasionally wool

WEFT
cotton, occasionally wool

PILE
thick, excellent-quality wool

ENDS
small kelim at both
ends with looped fringe at
one end, plain fringe
at the other

SIDES
single cord, overcast
with wool

WEAVER USING TIBETAN WEAVING TECHNIQUE

nations. Both New Zealand and Tibetan wool are used. Tibetan wool is usually hand-spun. Rugs are woven with both the asymmetrical and Tibetan knotting techniques. Both rug types are coarsely knotted with a thick pile.

Excellent-quality Swiss dyes are used in addition to natural dyes. During the 1970s several manufacturers began to produce vegetable-dyed carpets. This production was on a small scale and the carpets were more expensive than their chemically dyed counterparts; by the mid-1980s, production ceased. In the early 1990s, the weaving of vegetable-dyed carpets was begun again. These rugs are woven with old Tibetan patterns with hand-spun Tibetan wool.

Nepalese "Tibetan" carpets are woven with excellent-quality, hand-spun Tibetan wool. Copies of traditional Tibetan designs are produced in bright, saturated colors as well as with natural undyed wool. These designs include medallion designs, floral patterns, and animal patterns.

Shou, floral, and stylized dragon medallions are commonly used as well as snow lions, cranes, phoenix, and Buddhist ritual objects. Single or multiple medallions are woven, often with cloudband motifs in the field.

Many different border designs are used. The running-T, swastika, meandering-vine, and flower designs are the most common. Borders with abstract geometric patterns are also made. Some rugs have no border arrangement.

In addition to the traditional Tibetan patterns, the majority of rugs are woven with much simpler designs, such as an open field surrounded by a border or an open field with a stepped-fret motif in the corners surrounded by a border. In addition, a large number of rugs are woven with abstract geometric designs. These are woven primarily for the European markets.

The sizes woven in Nepalese carpets range from small mats to 9 feet 9 inches by 13 feet (3 by 4 meters). Runners, seat covers, and round carpets are also woven.

JAIL RUG, 7' x 10'

eleven

RUGS OF INDIA

The Mogul emperor Akbar brought the art of carpet weaving to India in the 16th century. He brought Persian weavers from Kashan, Isfahan, and Kerman to his imperial courts and established workshops for the weaving of carpets. These early Indian rugs were very similar to those of Persia in both design and weaving technique. Unfortunately, royal patronage of the Indian rug industry ended as the Mogul Empire began to break apart in the early 18th century.

In 1600, less than a hundred years after weaving was brought to India, British merchants established India's first carpet-weaving firm in Lahore (now in Pakistan). Other weaving workshops soon were established in Amritsar, Agra, and Delhi. The display of Indian carpets at the Great London Exhibition in 1851 created a new international interest in Indian carpets, and they soon became the vogue in Europe and North America. The demand was so great in the second half of the 19th century that prisoners were pressed into service to help meet the demand. The "jail" carpets they produced were world renowned for their excellent quality.

After India was granted independence in 1947, the new government took an active interest in the rug-weaving industry. The All India Handicrafts Board was formed in 1952 to help set high standards and develop the market and the enormous weaving potential. Students can learn the art of rug weaving at schools in Kashmir, Rajasthan, and Uttar Pradesh. Most of the rug weaving in India is done by men and small boys. Women and girls spin the wool and knot the fringes.

Chrome and acid dyes are used in Indian carpets. Chrome dyes, which are colorfast and will not fade when exposed to sunlight or washed with water, are used for the best-quality carpets. Acid dyes are used for carpets of lower quality.

Cotton, wool, and silk are the most important materials used in Indian carpets, the majority of which are woven with

RUG-WEAVING CENTERS OF NORTHERN INDIA

wool pile and cotton warp and weft threads. Both local Indian and imported New Zealand wool are used, with the best-quality rugs woven with imported wool or a blend of imported and local wools. Silk is used in some Persian-design carpets in order to accentuate and highlight certain motifs. Carpets made with silk pile are woven. Synthetic or "art silk" is also used in weaving.

The majority of Indian rugs are custom-made with specified designs, colors, sizes, and quality grades. Rug importers order and stock a "program line" of rugs with the same design but varying quality. The importers have trademarked names for each of their grades, making it difficult to differentiate qualities of rugs from different importers. When comparing rugs from different importers, an evaluation must be made on a direct analysis of the rugs.

To denote the Indian origin of rugs, the prefix "Indo" should precede the name. For example, a Kashan-design rug woven in India should be referred to as an "Indo-Kashan."

India's major carpet-weaving centers are in the provinces of Uttar Pradesh, Rajasthan, Kashmir, and Punjab. While carpets are woven in other areas scattered throughout northern India, their production is relatively small. There are approximately five hundred weaving villages and small towns in the province of Uttar Pradesh. The highest concentration of weaving is found in the Varanasi area, in Mirzapur, Bhadohi, and Allahabad.

JAIL CARPETS During the second half of the 19th century carpet weaving in jails was widespread throughout the Indian subcontinent. Numerous rugs were produced in the jails of Agra, Jaipur, Amritsar, Delhi, and Lahore.

Many of the designs used were floral patterns adapted from rugs of the Mogul period. Other designs were copied from Persian, Turkish, and Balouchi rugs. Floral lattice patterns, medallions, and repeated motifs were frequently woven. These carpets were woven in a wide range of sizes.

MIRZAPUR-BHADOHI The Mirzapur Bhadohi weaving area is located along the Ganges River in Uttar Pradesh. It

---

**JAIL
CARPETS**

◆

KNOT
asymmetrical

WARP
cotton

WEFT
cotton

PILE
wool

ENDS
kelim with knotted fringe
at both ends

SIDES
single cord, overcast
with wool

◆

MIRZAPUR-BHADOHI, 6' X 9'

MIRZAPUR-BHADOHI

KNOT
asymmetrical

WARP
cotton

WEFT
cotton

PILE
wool

ENDS
knotted fringe at
both ends

SIDES
single cord, overcast
with wool

JAIPUR

KNOT
asymmetrical

WARP
cotton

WEFT
one or two shoots, cotton

PILE
wool

ENDS
small kelim with knotted
fringe at both ends

SIDES
single cord, overcast
with wool

also includes the city of Allahabad. The area is responsible for the largest volume of carpets produced in India today. The weavers here are adept at weaving any design or color combination and even varying the tightness of the weave.

The rugs are woven with wool pile and cotton warps and wefts. Silk is occasionally used in the pile for highlights. This silk is usually artificial.

During the 1960s and '70s much of the production from this area was devoted to weaving carpets in Chinese and Aubusson designs. The majority of these rugs were rather coarsely woven. The pile was carved to accentuate the motifs and designs. Since the U.S. embargo was placed on rugs from Iran in the 1980s, the demand has been for finer-quality Persian design rugs to be woven. Many of these copies are similar in weave to the Persian originals. Their designs are well executed and the motifs are crisp and clear.

JAIPUR Jaipur is located 190 miles (306 kilometers) southwest of New Delhi in the state of Rajasthan. Jaipur is the state capital and the area's major center of carpet weaving.

Most of the weaving in Rajasthan is done in factories and workshops. The master weaver sits between two looms and calls out the pattern from a cartoon to the weavers sitting on the loom. Designs adopted from Iranian and Caucasian weaving centers are frequently used.

JAIPUR, 2' X 4'   AGRA, 4' X 6'

AGRA

◆

KNOT
asymmetrical

WARP
cotton

WEFT
one or two shoots, cotton

PILE
wool

ENDS
small kelim with knotted
fringe at both ends

SIDES
single cord, overcast
with wool

◆

The majority of Jaipur rugs have wool pile and cotton warp and weft threads. The wool used is durable and will withstand wear quite well. Local wool usually is blended with wool imported from New Zealand. Rajasthan is one of India's largest wool-producing areas. The blending of wools used in Jaipur yields stronger and more lustrous carpets.

AGRA The city of Agra is situated 125 miles (200 kilometers) southeast of New Delhi. Carpet weaving has been done here since the early 17th century and flourished under Mogul patronage.

During the 1930s copies of Sarouks intended for North American markets were woven with a central medallion and detached floral sprays on a red background. Currently patterns such as medallion-and-corner, repeated motifs, panels, and prayer designs reminiscent of Persian and Caucasian rugs are made. The fields of these rugs are crowded; they are filled with arabesques, trees, floral heads, and foliage. Other

KNOT
asymmetrical

WARP
cotton, silk

WEFT
cotton, silk

PILE
wool, silk, or artificial silk

ENDS
small kelim with knotted
fringe at both ends

SIDES
single cord, overcast with
wool or silk

◆

patterns used are inspired by carpets of the Mogul period and contain plant and tree motifs.

Agra rugs have wool pile and cotton warps and wefts. Silk occasionally is used to accentuate certain motifs. Much of the silk used is artificial, and is referred to as "art silk." A variety of color combinations are used, with multicolored motifs on a red or blue background or pastel-colored motifs on an ivory background. A wide range of sizes are available.

KASHMIR Carpet weaving has been done in Kashmir for more than four hundred years, but it was not until the late 19th century that a commercial industry began to develop. Currently many of India's finest carpets are woven in Kashmir. The finest qualities are produced in Srinagar.

In Kashmir, weavers use a *talim* instead of a cartoon in their weaving. A talim is a piece of paper on which the design has been written in script; it dictates the number of knots as well as the color combinations to be employed.

KASHMIR (SILK), 6' X 9'

KASHMIR (WOOL), 4' X 6'

Many of the designs used are adopted from Persian weaving centers. These designs are elaborate compositions, such as a central medallion design with a field crowded with flowers, palmettes, vines, and tendrils. Prayer designs woven in Kashmir also have fields filled with floral motifs. Adaptations of Kashmiri embroidery patterns are also woven.

Both wool and silk are used for the pile. Silk is often used as an accent in wool pile carpets. Wool pile rugs are woven on a cotton foundation and are given a luster wash to give a "silky" appearance to the pile. Silk pile rugs are woven with silk or cotton warps, depending on the quality. The finest-quality silk rugs are woven with silk warps. Synthetic or "art" silk is also used for pile. These artificial silk rugs are all too often sold to unsuspecting tourists as genuine silk rugs, and Kashmiri rugs with Persian designs often are misrepresented as genuine Persian rugs. Kashmiri rugs are woven in a wide range of sizes.

HIMACHAL PRADESH The mountainous state Himachal Pradesh is situated northwest of Uttar Pradesh and south of Kashmir. Himachal Pradesh is home-in-exile to the Dalai Lama and numerous other Tibetans who moved to the area in the 1960s. Much of the weaving here is done by Tibetan refugees. The weaving is basically a cottage industry carried on by women in Dharamsala, Manali, and other small towns in this state.

These carpets are typically Tibetan in design and structure. Designs frequently woven are dragons, snow lions, stylized chrysanthemums, and lotus flowers. Color combinations generally contain strong, bright shades of red, blue, yellow, green, and white. Some rugs are woven with undyed wool. The wool used is local Indian as well as Tibetan and other imported wool. The majority of carpets are woven in small sizes.

BACK OF KASHMIR (WOOL)

HIMACHAL

PRADESH

◆

KNOT
asymmetrical, or Tibetan
knotting technique

WARP
cotton

WEFT
cotton

PILE
wool, coarsely knotted

ENDS
small kelim with
knotted fringe

SIDES
single cord, overcast
with wool

◆

PAKISTANI RUG, PERSIAN DESIGN, 5' X 8'

twelve

RUGS OF PAKISTAN

akistan lies astride the ancient land route to the Indian

subcontinent and the Far East. The influences of migrations, invading armies, and trade have

left Pakistan with a rich culture which is visible in the arts and crafts of this region.

It is not known when the first carpets were woven in the Pakistan area, although it is

claimed that weaving was probably introduced by the ancient Scythians. In the 16th century

the Mogul emperor Akbar established carpet-weaving workshops in Lahore and Multan,

bringing Persian weavers to his imperial court. The carpets woven in these court workshops

were very similar to Persian rugs in weave as well as in the designs used. Soon a new Mogul

style began to emerge from the workshops, and in 1600 the East India Carpet Company was

founded in Lahore by British merchants for the express purpose of weaving Oriental carpets.

RUG-WEAVING CENTERS OF PAKISTAN

In 1947, Pakistan was created from the northwest areas of India when Britain granted independence to the Indian subcontinent. Religion was the major factor in the partitioning of Pakistan and India, Pakistan being mainly Muslim and India being mainly Hindu. At the time of the partitioning, many of the Muslim weavers moved from India to Lahore and other parts of Pakistan.

The new government in Pakistan recognized the need for industry and employment. Government subsidies were granted to the still-small Pakistani carpet-weaving industry, making the prices of their carpets very competitive in foreign markets. Soon Pakistan emerged as one of the world's leading manufacturers of Oriental carpets.

The greatest concentration of commercial weaving is done in and around the cities of Lahore, Karachi, and Peshawar. Many of the weaving areas have developed their own areas of specialization. Carpets are also woven in Afghan refugee camps; however, these carpets are Turkoman in structure and design (see page 127).

The majority of Pakistani rugs are woven for export. The

designs and color combinations of these rugs are dictated by foreign markets. Many Pakistani rugs are woven on a contract basis for European and North American importers. Manufacturers maintain a large repertory of designs and color combinations in varying qualities from which the foreign buyer may choose. In addition, buyers are able to request their own designs and colors.

An order usually is placed with a contractor for a specified number of rugs; the contractor will in turn subcontract a deal directly with the *ustad* (master weaver). The ustad will be given a cash advance, plus the wool and the design required. Weaving is done in homes and in "factories." Men and small boys do most of the weaving, while women and girls perform such duties as spinning the wool and knotting the fringes. A weaver will work eight hours a day, during which he will tie between 6,000 and 12,000 knots, depending on his skill and the difficulty of the design.

For the weaving of "Bukhara" (Turkoman-design) rugs, a cartoon is not used. Instead, the carpet pattern is translated into a type of shorthand. The shorthand contains a series of instructions that may be either woven by the weaver himself or called out to the weavers in chant by a master weaver. The master weaver is generally seated between two looms. Two or three weavers may work at a loom, each following the instructions called to them.

STRUCTURE Pakistani carpets generally are finely knotted with wool pile and cotton warp and weft threads. Silk and artificial silk are occasionally used in the pile to accentuate certain motifs. The asymmetrical knot is typically used.

The domestic wool is of good quality and is readily available. It is resilient, takes dye well, and is easily spun. However, the finest-quality carpets are woven with local wool that has been blended with merino wool imported from New Zealand, Korea, and Australia. This imported wool contains more lanolin, has a longer staple, and is stronger, yielding a more durable and lustrous carpet.

Good-quality chrome dyes are used. They are colorfast, and do not fade when exposed to light or bleed when washed.

MORI WEAVE

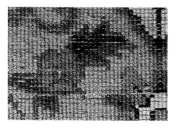

PERSIAN WEAVE

These dyes are easy to use both in their physical application and in the precise duplication of specific colors.

All rugs are given a chemical wash before export. Persian-design rugs are given a light chemical wash, and Bukhara-design rugs a "luster wash" to give the pile a silky texture.

Two types of weaves are used in Pakistani rugs: the *Mori* and the *Persian* weave. In both cases the quality or fineness of the weave is expressed by a set of numbers in the form of a fraction—for example, $\frac{9}{16}$ or $\frac{11}{22}$. The top figure is the number of horizontal knots in a linear inch; the bottom figure is the number of vertical knots in a linear inch. Thus, the number of knots per square inch is easily computed by multiplying the two figures together.

The Persian weave, used in rugs with Persian designs, resembles the back of Persian rugs with approximately the same number of vertical knots in a horizontal inch as in a vertical inch, although the number of horizontal knots per inch is slightly less than the number of vertical knots per inch. Persian-weave rugs may be woven with either single or double knots. The quality grades range from $\frac{13}{15}$ to $\frac{18}{20}$, with intermediate grades of $\frac{14}{16}$ and $\frac{16}{18}$.

The Mori weave characteristically is woven in rugs with Turkoman or Caucasian designs. Asymmetrical knots may be tied in a single or a double knot on warp threads that are on the same level. Double-knotted rugs (referred to as "doubles") have two strands of knotted wool. Carpets of this type are thicker and have a longer pile than the single-knotted ones. Double-knotted carpets are usually contracted for in the $\frac{9}{16}$ grade.

(The use of the term "double knot" is somewhat ambiguous. It is most often used to mean two strands of yarn tied around the same pair of warp threads or, less frequently, to refer to the symmetrical knot, where a strand of wool makes two loops, one loop around each of the warp threads.)

The wool used for the pile of both single- and double-knotted rugs may be either single or double ply. The quality of the double-ply rugs will range from $\frac{8}{12}$ to $\frac{8}{18}$, with intermediate grades of $\frac{8}{14}$, $\frac{9}{14}$, and $\frac{9}{16}$; the single-ply rugs have quality grades of $\frac{11}{22}$, $\frac{11}{24}$, and $\frac{12}{22}$.

BUKHARA

◆

KNOT
asymmetrical

WARP
cotton

WEFT
two shoots, cotton

PILE
wool; silk occasionally
used for highlights

ENDS
small kelim with knotted
fringe at both ends

SIDES
single cord, overcast
with wool

◆

PAKISTANI BUKHARA,
4' X 6'

DESIGNS Designs woven in Pakistani rugs have been adopted from designs of other weaving centers. The "Bukhara" design was adopted from Turkoman rugs; numerous other designs have been borrowed from the weaving centers of the Caucasus, Turkey, and Iran. The designers of Pakistani carpets also are adept at creating new designs.

The "Bukhara" or Turkoman-design Pakistani rug is the most popular and widely known on the market. For several decades it was the mainstay of the Pakistani rug business. The Bukhara rug has evolved from the early thick-pile prototypes with coarse wool and a narrow range of colors. Currently numerous Turkoman designs and adaptations of traditional Turkoman designs are woven in Pakistani rugs. The quality grades vary from medium to very finely woven.

The use of color in Turkoman-design carpets is rather limited; usually only two or three colors are used. In traditional Turkoman weavings, red is the predominant color; however, Pakistani Bukharas use numerous color combinations as dictated by foreign demand.

The Caucasian designs most copied are those of Kazak, Kuba, and Shirvan. These rugs are woven with geometric medallions and motifs in bright shades of red, blue, and white. Pastel-colored motifs are also used with an ivory background.

Since the 1980s U.S. embargo of Iranian carpets, the production of Persian-design Pakistani rugs has increased dramatically to fill the American void of fine-quality Persian rugs such as Isfahan, Nain, Kashan, and Kerman. The quality of Pakistani Persian-design rugs has greatly improved. Many rugs are woven with merino wool and intricate designs that compare in quality with a Kashan or Isfahan rug woven in Iran. A wide variety of Persian designs are used. The color combinations are esthetically pleasing and not harsh. In many of the finer-woven carpets the motifs are outlined in the same manner as the finer Persian rugs.

Prayer design rugs adopted from Turkish weaving centers are also produced. The Ghiordes prayer rug was one of the first designs adopted for use in Pakistani rugs. Prayer rugs are made in small mat sizes. In addition, the *saff*, multiple-niche prayer rug is woven with as many as nine niches placed side by side.

ROMANIAN RUG, BUCHARESTI QUALITY, 4' x 6'

thirteen

RUGS OF ROMANIA

omania is situated in southeastern Europe; it

borders Ukraine on the north, Hungary on the northwest, Yugoslavia on the southwest, Bulgaria on

the south, and the Black Sea and Moldavia on the east. Moldavia was part of Romania until it

was ceded to the Soviet Union after World War II. In land area, Romania can be compared

with England or the state of Oregon. Ninety percent of the population is Romanian; ethnic

minorities include Hungarians, Germans, Armenians, Serbs, Gypsies, Turks, and Ukrainians.

Hand-knotted carpets arrived in Romania as early as the Middle Ages through the trade

routes and trading with the Romanian principalities. Customs documents of Brasov mention

that more than five hundred Persian and Turkish carpets were imported between January 7

and November 6, 1503. In Brasov, the Black Church has a very fine collection of Turkish and

RUG-WEAVING AREAS OF ROMANIA

Transylvanian carpets of the 17th and 18th centuries. This collection of approximately 120 carpets includes Lotto, Ushak, Ladik, Kula, Ghiordes, as well as a few 19th-century Caucasian rugs.

Hand-knotted carpets have been woven in Romania for more than three hundred years. Archives in Braila and Galati document that carpets were woven in these two cities for over two hundred years. The structure and design of the early Romanian carpets were influenced by the Armenian and Turkish traders and merchants who imported rugs into Romania.

By the beginning of the 20th century, the weaving of pile carpets was well established in the towns of Bucharest, Galati, Braila, Craiova, Oradea, Iasi, Cluj, and Harman. Although early carpet production was rather limited, the carpets woven were of excellent quality.

One of the most notable Romanian workshops of the 20th century was that of Theodor Tuduc. His workshops in Brasov until 1945, and after World War II in Bucharest, were famous for their copies of Turkish and Transylvanian carpets. An expert restorer and weaver, Tuduc also copied European carpets and post-conquest South American weavings.* Several of Tuduc's more infamous works were purchased by museums,

*Ian Bennet. "All that Glisters," *Hali* 48 (1989), 96–98.

including London's Victoria and Albert and the Berlin Museum.

After World War I, many Armenians immigrated to Romania and other Balkan countries from their traditional homeland in eastern Anatolia. Many of these immigrants were expert weavers and established workshops for the weaving of carpets. One such workshop in Braila was reported to have had more than three hundred weavers between 1925 and 1930. S. H. Cascanian, an Armenian refugee, was instrumental in advising and setting up the craft cooperatives throughout Romania. He helped organize Cartimex, for the exportation of carpets, and assisted in the overseas marketing organization ICECOOP.

Since the early 1950s, carpet weaving in Romania has become standardized. More than 15,000 weavers are employed in handicraft cooperatives throughout the country. Their activities are guided and coordinated by the Central Board of the Folk Art and Artistic Handicrafts of the Central Union of Handicrafts Cooperative (UCECOM). Cooperatives in Bucharest, Braila, Harman, Galati, Oradea, Tulcea, and Focsani specialize solely in the production of hand-knotted carpets. There are seventy additional departments for the weaving of hand-knotted carpets in other cooperatives throughout Romania. A round, numbered metal tag denotes the cooperative where the rug was woven.

Women do the weaving in these cooperatives and in small workshops. In some areas, rugs are woven by individuals in their homes; a small number are woven in workshops set up in monasteries and convents.

The majority of hand-knotted rugs woven in Romania are produced under contract with rug importers and wholesalers. The contract calls for a designated number of carpets to be delivered within a certain amount of time. Designs, color combinations, sizes, and qualities are specified by the importer. Special requests for new designs, adaptations in old designs, and color combinations are regularly taken.

STRUCTURE Romanian rugs are woven on vertical looms with either a steel or a wooden frame. The looms are well engineered, enabling the weaver to produce a carpet with straight sides. Looms are normally set up for carpets up to 3 meters wide but can accommodate those up to 5 meters in width.

One of the distinguishing features of Romanian carpets is the uniform appearance of the back. The variations in knot sizes, normally visible on the back of hand-knotted rugs, are so slight that the rug seems almost machine made.

With the exception of the designs woven in Transylvanian carpets of the 17th and 18th centuries, there are no designs associated with a town or indigenous to an area in Romania. For centuries Romanian rug designs have been adopted and adapted from the weaving centers of the Caucasus, Persia, and Turkey. More than five hundred designs and adaptations of traditional designs are found in Romania carpets. In many instances the design is better executed than in the original rug. Romanian weavers are capable of weaving virtually any design and expanding it into any proportion.

The turcana and merino wool used for the pile is almost exclusively from Romanian sheep. It is of an excellent quality, resilient, and hard-wearing. The sheep are pastured in the Carpathian Mountains in the summer and in the winter they graze in the Danube delta area of Dobrogea. After shearing, the wool is sent to spinning mills for carding, combing, and spinning.

Dyeing is done in several cooperatives by computerized machines, recently purchased from Germany, which wash the wool, removing the grease, and do the dyeing. In the dyeing process, the wool is also mothproofed. These machines are capable of uniform dyeing and matching of different dye lots. Chrome dyes are used which are colorfast and will not fade when washed or exposed to sunlight. Many of the larger carpet factories have their own dye houses, but generally the wool is dyed in Bucharest.

All Romanian carpets receive a light chemical wash before export. This opens the tips of the knots and gives the pile a brighter appearance. The larger cooperatives have their own facilities for doing this; the smaller ones send their carpets to the large establishments in Bucharest.

The quality of Romanian rugs is determined primarily by

the knot count, according to which the quality is standardized into several distinct grades. Grades range from 40,000 knots per square meter to 360,000. All Romanian rugs are labeled with a tag denoting quality. However, if this tag is not present, it is quite easy to determine the quality by simply counting the knots per square inch. The names given to the different quality grades are also names of towns and areas; however, there is no relationship between the two. Bucharest-quality rugs are woven throughout Romania, in Braila, Brasov, and other cooperatives as well as in Bucharest itself.

Romanian hand-knotted rugs are divided into two types: those woven with cotton warp and weft threads and asymmetrical knots and those with wool warp and weft threads and symmetrical knots. The Harman II quality is the exception. These rugs are woven with cotton warp and wool wefts with a symmetrical knot. The terminal knots on both sides of all Romanian rugs are woven with symmetrical knots.

The majority of all cotton-foundation rugs are woven in the Bucharesti quality. They are made with a good-quality wool and will withstand wear as well as or better than any other rugs with a comparable knot count. They are reasonably priced and provide a good, inexpensive floor covering. A variety of designs are woven, Tabriz and Herez patterns being some of the most popular. All sizes are made, from small mats to runners and room-size rugs.

The Braila quality is woven with more intricate patterns than the Bucharesti quality. Excellent copies of Persian Mud rugs in a repeated Herati pattern with a central medallion are well executed, and the designs are crisp and clear. Designs commonly used are the medallion-and-corner, Herati, Boteh, and Shah Abbas and are adopted from the weaving centers of Kashan, Isfahan, Qum, Tabriz, Sarouk, and Mud.

Mures-quality rugs are finely woven with merino wool. Designs have intricate motifs and patterns reminiscent of the Persian weaving centers of Sarouk, Kashan, Tabriz, and Mashad.

Transylvania-quality rugs are woven with wool warp and weft threads. Like the Bucharesti quality, they are woven with a good quality of wool and withstand wear very well. The color combinations and designs are beautifully executed copies of

BACK OF ROMANIAN RUG,
BUCHARESTI QUALITY

ROMANIAN RUG, TRANSYLVANIA QUALITY, 9' X 12'

Caucasian and Turkish carpets. These rugs come in a variety of sizes.

Brasov-quality rugs contain more intricate motifs and designs than Transylvania-quality rugs. Many of the designs are copies of 18th- and 19-century Turkish and Caucasian rugs. Brasov-quality rugs are woven in a variety of different sizes.

Harman-quality rugs are woven only in the Harman cooperative, which specializes in the weaving of copies of antique Caucasian, Persian, and French Savonnerie rugs. The designs and colors are similar to those found in antique carpets. The ability to reproduce the soft, muted colors is a specialty of the Harman cooperative as well as a closely guarded secret. These tones are obtained in the dyeing process and not by chemical washing of the carpet. Any "antique wash" given to a Harman rug is done after it has been exported from Romania. Harman-quality rugs come in a variety of sizes, from small carpets to runners and large room-size rugs.

The Harman cooperative produces beautifully executed copies of the old Persian Herez patterns. These rugs are often woven in the Harman II quality, with cotton warp threads, excellent-quality wool pile, and soft colors. This quality is similar to antique Herez rugs in structure and design. Herez-design rugs are woven in large room sizes, 6 by 9 feet (183 by 274 centimeters) and larger.

QUALITY GRADES OF ROMANIAN CARPETS		
QUALITY GRADE	KNOTS PER SQUARE METER	KNOTS PER SQUARE INCH
COTTON FOUNDATION		
Dorna	40,000	25
Bucharesti	108,900	70
Braila	160,000	103
Mures	200,000	129
Olt	250,000	160
Milcov	300,000	194
Calatis	360,000	232
WOOL FOUNDATION		
Nomad	92,000	59
Timpa	75,000	48
Bran	92,400	60
Transylvania	121,600	79
Brasov	160,000	103
Harman I	200,000	129
Postavarul	240,000	155
COTTON WARP/ WOOL WEFT		
Harman II	200,000	129

ROMANIAN KELIM, TISMANA QUALITY, 4' X 6'

fourteen

PILELESS RUGS AND FLAT WEAVES

ileless rugs are the oldest and most widespread form of handmade carpets. They are woven on both upright and horizontal looms, similar to those used in the weaving of pile carpets. Flat weaves and pileless rugs are woven in a number of different techniques. They are known by different names depending on their structural characteristics and where they are woven. Kelim, soumak, jajim, zili, cicim, dhurrie, and scoarta are all types of pileless weaving.

TYPES OF WEAVES

The simplest form of flat weave is a *plain weave*. The warp and weft threads are evenly interwoven, with the warps and wefts equally visible. This type of weave is used as the background weave for zili and verneh weaves.

PLAIN WEAVE

VERNEH WITH PLAIN WEAVE

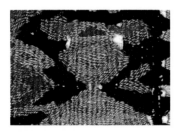

SLIT WEAVE

SHARED WARP

SOUMAK

A *kelim*, or tapestry weave, is a weft-faced weave created by passing the wefts back and forth over and under the warps, completely covering them. Designs are formed by using different-colored wefts. There are several types of kelim weaving, depending on the method used at the juncture of two different-colored wefts: the slit weave, shared warp, and interlocking wefts. In the *slit-weave* (slit-tapestry) technique, the two colors are kept separate, so that each colored weft doubles back on itself, creating a slit at the juncture. In the *shared-warp* (dovetail) technique, the colored wefts meet and share a common warp; the colored wefts loop around the warp and double back on themselves. The *interlocking-wefts* technique has colored wefts that meet and interlock, loop around each other, and double back on their own color. A *double interlocking-wefts* technique has colored wefts that interlock with two loops instead of one.

A *soumak* is woven with a weft-wrapping technique by which a supplementary colored weft is used to create a motif or design area. The colored weft is wrapped around the warps, passing over four warps, under two, over four, and under two in sequence, similar to a chain stitch. The supplementary colored wefts completely cover the foundation wefts.

A *jajim* is a warp-faced weave, woven in long narrow strips. After the weaving process has been completed, desired lengths of jajim are cut and sewn together selvedge to selvedge. The ends are hemmed and turned under.

DECORATIVE TECHNIQUES

Various decorative techniques are used in combination with plain and kelim weaves. They may be done on the loom, called a *weft float*, or added once the carpet has been removed, called an *embroidery*.

The *weft float (brocade)* is a weaving technique whereby an extra weft is used to create a surface pattern or motif. As a motif is finished, the yarn is pulled across or "floated" across the back of the rug between the pattern areas before another motif is started. Weft floats can be several different techniques, for example the *zili* and *cicim*.

A *zili* is a pileless weaving technique in which an extra weft

JAJIM

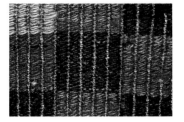

ZILI

floats on a plain weave. The extra weft float splits a pair of warps and is laid over and under the warp threads. The surface of the weave is completely covered with floats over two, three, or five warps.

A *cicim* is a weft-float weaving technique in which an additional colored weft is interlaced into the regular warp and weft system. The motifs have the appearance of solid lines over the ground weave.

An *embroidery* is a type of decoration which is done after the weaving process has been completed. The design or motif is added to the textile with a needle.

Flat weaves and pileless carpets are woven in Iran, Turkey, the Caucasus, Turkestan, Afghanistan, Pakistan, India, and Eastern Europe. They are used as floor coverings, eating cloths, cradles, blankets, storage bags, saddlebags, and animal trappings.

IRAN

Pileless carpets, bags, and animal trappings are woven by virtually all of the tribal groups in Iran. Much of the weaving is done by nomads and seminomads as well as by those who lead a settled existence. The designs and patterns used are predominately geometric, with rectilinear motifs and figures. Senna and Bijar kelims are the exception; they are woven with curvilinear designs.

QASHQA'I WOMAN WEAVING A KELIM ON A HORIZONTAL LOOM

KELIMS *Senna* kelims are woven in the town of Sanandaj by Kurdish weavers. Senna kelims are woven with the slit-tapestry technique and are considered to be among the best examples of pileless weaving. They are finely woven with thin cotton warps. Their designs are refined, delicate, and small-scale compared to those used in other kelims. The most common design employed by these weavers is a central medallion superimposed on a field filled with the repeated Herati motif, similar to Senna pile carpets. Prayer designs are woven with either a repeated Herati or Boteh pattern.

Bijar kelims are woven in and around the town of Bijar. Bijar kelims, like Sennas, are made by Kurdish villagers but they are not as finely woven. The bodies of Bijar kelims are thicker and

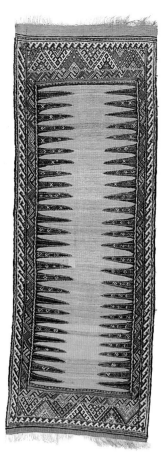

the designs are not as finely executed.

Kurds, both nomadic and seminomadic, also weave pileless carpets as well as saddle and storage bags. Kurdish kelims are woven in an elongated format in a slit-tapestry technique, often with additional weft outlining. Kurdish bags commonly are woven with a mixed technique, for example a soumak weave for the face of the bag and a kelim for the back.

Shiraz. Currently inexpensive kelims are commercially woven in the Shiraz area. These kelims, collectively known as Shiraz kelims, are woven by Persian villagers as well as settled tribal weavers. The Shiraz kelims are relatively thick and are coarsely woven in the slit-tapestry technique. The designs are composed of repeated geometric motifs and geometric medallions. Both cotton and wool are used for the warps. The colors are white, blue, golden yellow, brick red, and blue.

Qashqa'i weavers produce kelims for floor coverings, blankets, animal trappings, and storage bags. The designs used in Qashqa'i kelims are not as elaborate as those used in the weaving of pile carpets. Common designs include multicolored diagonal stripes, horizontal bands, central medallion, and an empty field surrounded by a series of borders. Qashqa'i kelims are finely woven with the slit-tapestry technique. In addition to their traditional kelims, the Qashqa'i currently are weaving Gabbeh-

QASHQA'I SALT BAG, 1'6" X 1'6"   GABBEH KELIM, 5' X 7'9"

like kelims. These kelims are finely woven with natural dyes in beautiful shades of blue, green, yellow, and red. The designs are simple: geometric medallions with large expanses of open field. Animal and human figures are frequently interspersed throughout the field.

Balouchi weavers are prolific producers of kelims, flat-woven storage bags, and animal trappings. The Balouchi also use a combination of pile and kelim weaving in the same piece. The *sofreh* (eating cloth), for example, has the motif portion woven in a pile technique and the ground of the cloth, in weft-faced tapestry weave. In their pileless weavings, the Balouchi often use a combination of weft wrapping and weft-float brocading. A common design used in bags is alternating dark and light stripes.

JAJIMS Jajims are woven by various tribal groups in Iran for use as bedding, storage bags, floor coverings, and animal trappings. The Iran Handicrafts Organization produces long rolls of jajims in various regions throughout Iran.

SOUMAKS Soumaks are currently woven in the Eastern Azerbaijan province around the towns of Serab and Ardebil; they are often called Ardebil soumaks on the market. These soumaks are woven with cotton warps and wool ground wefts.

The design wefts are wool or a combination of wool and silk; wool is used for the designs, and silk for the background. Some of the soumaks are given a chemical wash to give them an aged appearance. They are woven primarily in small sizes, up to 4 by 6 feet (120 by 180 centimeters). The designs employed are geometric, usually a central medallion with small chickens, birds, lions, and human figures scattered throughout the field. The colors commonly used are red, light and dark blue, burnt orange, white, and yellow. In the Kerman province, Afshars currently weave soumaks in sizes up to 5 by 8 feet (150 by 245 centimeters). Afshar soumaks are woven with wool design wefts in colors primarily of blue, red, and white. The designs employed include that of a central geometric medallion and repeated geometric motifs.

In addition to floor covering, the soumak weaving technique is used for the faces of storage bags, salt bags, and cradles. This weft-wrapping technique is used by virtually all of the tribal groups in Iran.

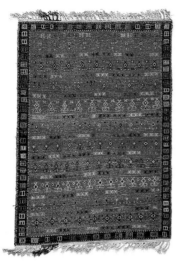

GABBEH SOUMAK, 5' X 8'

THE CAUCASUS

KELIMS are often referred to in the Caucasus as *palas*. Kelims with a repeated shield motif on a dark-blue or red field are associated with the Kuba area. The kelims with a blue field have an ivory border and those with a red field have either a dark-brown or blue border. The main border design is composed of either a meander-and-bar pattern or a zigzag stripe punctuated by a bar. Kelims in which the field is divided into a series of horizontal bands of contrasting colors, with each band containing a hexagonal motif or a latch-hook motif, are associated with the Shirvan area. Kelims of this type have no border arrangement.

VERNEH BAG, 3' X 4'

VERNEH are woven in the Moghan steppe and in northern Iran primarily by the Shahsavan. Verneh are woven on a plain ground weave with an added weft wrapping used for the designs and motifs. The patterns most often used in the field composition are repeated flowers, trees, stars, or small geometric motifs. Birds and animal figures also appear. Verneh are usually woven in narrow strips and sewn together in various widths as the requirements dictate. When used as floor coverings, they are quite often lined with felt for reinforcement. In addition to floor or ground covers, Vernehs are used as eating cloths, bedding, storage bags, and horse and camel covers.

SOUMAKS The weaving of Soumaks was once attributed to the town of Shemakha, capital of the Shirvan province. This type of weaving, however, was probably more widespread than just this area. Soumak weaving has been attributed to Kuba, Daghestan, and Karabagh, and is currently practiced in Armenia. Caucasian Soumaks are woven in the "countered" soumak technique (alternating rows in different directions), giving a herringbone effect. When the colored weft is changed, the thread is pulled through to the back of the carpet and left to hang.

A common design used in Soumak rugs is that of two or three blue, notched, lozenge-shaped medallions on a brick-red field interspersed with stars, rosettes, human figures, and a variety of small motifs. The main border is either a Seishour-type bird's head border or a repeated rosette on a blue background. The warp and weft threads are of wool. The sizes range from 4 by 7 feet (120 by 215 centimeters) to 6 feet 6 inches by 9 feet 9 inches (2 by 3 meters).

ERZURUM, 4' X 6'

SILEH are usually woven in two panels that are joined after the weaving process has been completed. They are made with wool warp and ground weft threads. The design consists of rows of large repeated S motifs, derivative of a dragon motif. Within each large S are small repeated S motifs. Silehs are woven with a soumak technique. The only border is narrow and consists of a reciprocal pattern. Silehs are usually made in large sizes.

TURKEY

KELIMS The majority of Turkish kelims are woven in the slit-tapestry technique, with the motifs outlined by an extra strand of yarn wrapped around the warp threads. This outlining serves several purposes: it covers the slits formed by the juncture of the two colored weft threads, and it accentuates the designs and motifs.

Turkish kelims come in a variety of sizes, from small mats to long narrow rugs. They are generally woven on narrow looms, which limits the width of the kelim. Old Turkish kelims frequently were woven in two strips and sewn together. Some modern kelims are woven on wider looms in one piece.

The designs used in Turkish kelims vary depending on the area where the kelim was woven. The Prayer design is one of the most common patterns used; the shape and size of the prayer arch varies according to the area it comes from. Other designs frequently used include concentric medallions, repeated hexagonal medallions, and latch-hook motifs.

OUTLINING WITH EXTRA
STRAND OF YARN

CICIM AND ZILI techniques are also employed by Turkish weavers. The pieces are woven by the nomads for animal covers, storage bags, and small rugs. Many were produced by Yuruks.

TURKESTAN

Pileless Turkoman weaving generally consists of a combination of several different techniques. Mixed techniques are found in storage bags, tent bands, animal trappings, and floor coverings woven by most Turkoman tribes. Traditionally the

YOMUD CHUVAL, 2'6" X 5'

Yomud, Tekke, and Ersari were the most prolific weavers of pileless carpets and textiles.

Turkomans rarely weave plain kelims. They often combine a plain weave with a weft-float brocade used in the borders. Turkoman weavers frequently use brocades on a plain weave, weft wrapping, weft-float brocades, and the interlocking-tapestry technique. Jajims are also woven.

Repeated patterns of guls and geometric motifs are most commonly used. The palette is rather limited, with red used for the background and white, blue, and black for the motifs. The white is quite often cotton, since the supply of white wool is limited. The black is natural dark-colored wool.

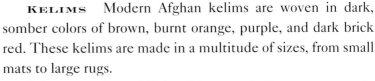

AFGHANISTAN

In Afghanistan, pileless weaving is done in a variety of different techniques by Turkomans, Balouchi, Uzbeks, Afghans, Tadzhiks, Pastuns, and other ethnic groups. The weavings produced by each of these groups reflect its ethnic origin in structure and design.

BALOUCHI BAG

KELIMS Modern Afghan kelims are woven in dark, somber colors of brown, burnt orange, purple, and dark brick red. These kelims are made in a multitude of sizes, from small mats to large rugs.

A large number of Balouchi prayer kelims are woven in Afghanistan, with designs similar to those of Balouchi pile rugs. Common are a rectilinear prayer arch with a stylized Tree-of-Life design or repeated geometric motifs filling the field. The colors are somber shades of blue, brown, rust, caramel, and white.

DHURRIES Finely woven dhurries with cotton warp and weft threads are woven in jails as well as by individuals in their homes in various parts of Afghanistan. Excellent-quality dhurries were produced by convicts in Mazar-i-Sharif. They are woven in soft pastel colors in a variety of sizes up to very large formats. Finely woven cotton dhurries are more expensive than wool kelims.

In India, weft-faced pileless rugs are known as dhurries. Originally they were woven entirely of cotton, but since the late 1940s wool has been used for the wefts. Today the majority of dhurries are woven with wool wefts and cotton warps. Those of the finest quality come from the Agra, Srinagar, and Bhadohi areas. Finer-quality dhurries are woven with a blend of local, New Zealand, and Australian wool. The imported wool yields a stronger carpet and gives a more lustrous appearance. Wool dhurries are produced primarily in the Bhadohi area and cotton dhurries in Srinagar and Agra. In Agra, gold and silk threads are added to accentuate certain motifs. A few all-silk dhurries are produced and are expensive.

Designs woven in dhurries tend to be geometric. Floral patterns are linear and do not have intricate, curved outlines. Central medallions, stripes, repeated floral sprays or geometric motifs, abstract modern designs, and stylized animal, bird, and human figures are all used.

DHURRIE, 6' x 6'

Dhurries are woven with the shared-warp technique. They are either finished with fringe at both ends or bound on all four sides with a wool overcasting, and are completely reversible. Dhurries are inexpensive but attractive floor coverings and come in all sizes, from small mats to room-size rugs.

A *drugget* is a coarsely woven, inexpensive flat weave. The wool used for the weft is not combed well before spinning and is often mixed with other fibers. The designs are simple geometric patterns. Druggets are woven in small sizes, 3 by 5 feet (90 by 150 centimeters), 4 by 6 feet (120 by 180 centimeters), and 5 by 7 feet (150 by 215 centimeters).

CHINA

In China, kelims are made with wool wefts and cotton warps. They are finely woven with the shared-warp technique. The Chinese use an excellent-quality wool which is softer than that used in most other kelims.

Both geometric and floral designs are used in Chinese kelims. Copies of Indian dhurries have geometric designs in pastel colors. Floral patterns reminiscent of Bessarabian kelims are also found. These kelims are finely woven with multicolored floral bouquets on dark- or light-colored backgrounds. Other patterns woven are reminiscent of French Aubusson designs.

ROMANIA

Kelims have played an important and practical role in the everyday life of Romanian peasants. Traditionally their homes were filled with kelims and woven textiles. Two types of kelims were woven in Romania, *scoarte* and *laicerul*. Both were made with the slit-tapestry technique.

Scoarte were used as table carpets, bed and seat covers, as well as floor coverings. These kelims contain design elements that reflect both Romanian folk art and a Turkish influence. *Laicerul* were used as wall covers; they were hung along the wall by a large transverse beam. Both decorative and functional, they helped insulate against the cold. The designs woven in this type of kelim were simple, either stripes filled with small geometric motifs, or simple geometric designs. There was no border arrangement.

Oltenian kelims are considered to be the finest of the Romanian kelims. Their designs are more floral in character than those of most kelims, containing curving flower and leaf sprays. Oltenian weavers developed a special talent for weaving these curved designs and motifs by using an eccentric way of weft beating. Designs of elongated branches of leaves and flowers are used, along with the traditional colors of cherry red, blue, black, white, and green. The background of the field is usually dark-colored, with white used for the border.

Moldavian kelims are somber, woven in shades of black, gray, green, and brown. Striped patterns with small floral motifs and a stylized Tree-of-Life pattern are characteristic. The floral designs woven in Moldavian kelims are more stylized than those used in Oltenia, and the borders are narrower.

Bessarabian kelims are from a part of Romania that is now part of the Ukraine. These kelims have curvilinear floral patterns; however, their patterns are more formal, sophisticated, and elaborate than those found in other areas of southeast Europe. The colors typically used are bright red and yellow gold with a black or dark-colored background. Bessarabian kelims are found in relatively large sizes, and occasionally contain inscriptions in the Cyrillic alphabet.

Currently kelims are produced in handicraft cooperatives throughout Romania. They are woven on both horizontal and vertical looms with turcana and merino wool from Romanian sheep. The slit-tapestry and shared-warp techniques are used, depending on the quality of the kelim.

Wool used in kelim weaving is treated differently than that used in the weaving of pile carpets. In the initial washing most of the natural oil is removed, yielding a whiter wool. Acid dyes are used which yield bright and clear colors. After the weaving is completed the kelim is removed from the loom, the fuzzy woolen hairs are trimmed with scissors, then the kelim is ironed with a damp cloth. Kelims are not chemically washed.

Both geometric and floral designs are woven in modern Romanian kelims. In addition to a wide variety of standard designs, numerous designs and patterns are made to order.

IRINA KELIM, 6'6" X 9'9"

The quality of Romanian kelims is determined by the tightness of weave. There are six quality grades of kelims: Carpati, Dorna, Tismana, Romanesc, Ileana, and Irina. The majority of kelims produced are woven in the Carpati, Tismana, and Irina qualities.

Carpati kelims are woven with geometric designs and patterns. This quality is woven on horizontal looms with either wool or cotton warps. The cooperative in Tirgoviste specializes in their production. Carpati kelims are inexpensive and can be compared in quality to modern Shiraz kelims.

Tismana is the medium-quality grade of Romanian kelims and the most popular. The largest percentage of Romanian kelims are woven in this quality. Tismana kelims are woven on vertical looms in numerous cooperatives. Most of the patterns used in this quality are floral, reminiscent of traditional Oltenian patterns. They are woven in traditional Olt colors of red, blue, and white as well as new color combinations in beautiful pastel shades for foreign markets (see page 192).

The *Irina* is the finest quality of Romanian kelim. Its intricate floral patterns are reminiscent of the Bessarabian kelims and tapestry-type weaves. Irina kelims are woven with merino wool with as many as fifty different shades used in one kelim. Irina kelims are expensive, though their excellent quality justifies their price.

SHOPPING FOR AN ORIENTAL RUG

fifteen

BUYING AN ORIENTAL RUG

riental rugs are beautiful and one of the most practical home furnishings you can buy. Their rich colors and design enhance any interior and create a warm feeling for someone entering a room.

Purchasing an Oriental rug should be a pleasurable experience for the first-time buyer. Do not be frustrated by the unusual-sounding names, different color combinations, designs, and ranges of rug quality. Group or categorize rugs by country of origin, tribal group or town where they are made. Make several trips to local Oriental rug shops before you buy and take notes about the rugs you like, for example, old Persian rugs woven with a medallion design in soft colors. When you are making your final selection, remember that each rug should be evaluated on its own merits, considering its condition, age, size, design, price, and country of origin.

An Oriental rug should be purchased as a work of art. Unfortunately, there are no absolutes that govern your choice. There are, however, some basic guidelines that you should follow and questions that you should keep in mind.

Establish a minimum and maximum dimension suitable for the intended use of the rug. Rug sizes are quoted from pile end to pile end, not including the fringe; so if you have a limited area to cover, make sure to allow for the fringe.

Keep in mind the upper limit that you are willing to spend and avoid buying a more expensive rug than the intended use warrants.

WHERE TO BUY

There are numerous sources from which to buy an Oriental rug. The most common are Oriental rug dealers, antique dealers, auctions, private sales, and foreign bazaars.

ORIENTAL RUG DEALERS Established and reputable Oriental rug dealers are the single best and most reliable source. They are able to advise you on the wearing qualities, investment potential, and care of your Oriental rug. The final appraisal and decision, however, lies with the purchaser.

Some dealers may tend to specialize in rugs of a particular county, a particular range of sizes (carrying mostly room-size rugs, for example), or a narrow price range (either at the low end for volume of sales or the high end for investors and collectors). However, most dealers do carry a wide selection of rugs in a variety of sizes and price ranges. It is advisable to visit all the rug shops in your area to gain a better view of what is available across the broad range of rugs you will encounter.

Choosing an Oriental rug dealer may be a problem for the first-time buyer. It may come down to buying from the dealer who has a rug you want. The careful buyer considers the reputation of the dealer. Word-of-mouth advertising and the recommendations of satisfied customers, especially those who have made several rug purchases, should be given weight.

BUYING AT AUCTION Many people are lured by the excitement of buying at auction. The hope of obtaining an Oriental rug for a fraction of its worth brings thousands of prospective buyers to auctions each year. The knowledgeable buyer may be able to make some good acquisitions, making careful selections from the wide range of rugs offered.

Buying an Oriental rug at any auction entails risks; the degree of risk varies with the kind of auction and the knowledge of the buyer. The successful buyer not only has knowledge of rugs but also is familiar with the procedures and requirements of the auction. No rug purchased at an auction is returnable; the buyer rarely has any recourse if the rug is not as represented, if it is in need of repair, or if the buyer decides that he or she simply does not like it. It is difficult to properly inspect the condition of a rug, and rugs are sold on an "as is" basis.

Before buying a rug at any auction, there are a few questions that should be kept in mind:

- What is the provenance of the rug?
- What is the actual value of the rug?
- What would a comparable rug cost in an Oriental rug store?
- What is the condition?
- What repairs are needed?
- What will necessary repairs cost?

If you are in doubt about the authenticity and value of a rug, it is advisable to pay for an independent appraisal. For example, "Tabriz design" or "Tabriz type" implies that the rug is woven in Iran. Copies of Persian Tabriz rugs are woven in Pakistan, Romania, and India and sell for much less than the originals. Any certificate that is given with the purchase should have the country of origin clearly stated.

There are three types of auctions: traveling or itinerant, estate, and those held at established auction houses. Each has its own attributes and benefits, as well as disadvantages.

Traveling/itinerant auctions go from city to city, selling Oriental rugs in motels or other rented facilities. The auctioneers are master showmen and may have "shills" (their hired people in the audience) to bid the price up until an acceptable level has been reached. The rug will not be sold for less than a predetermined price that recovers all costs and yields a profit. Such costs include rent of the facility, auctioneer's commission, transportation costs, plus the cost of each rug.

A common misconception of the auction is that all rugs must be sold regardless of price. In the traveling auction, the auctioneer is under no such pressure. If the bids do not exceed the auctioneer's minimum, that rug is withdrawn, to be offered again in the next city on the circuit. The risk is placed on the potential buyer, not on the auctioneer. Only on rare occasions is one able to purchase a rug for an amount less than its worth.

Many of the rugs sold at traveling auctions are rugs that for one reason or another do not sell on the wholesale market, or are wholesalers' rejects. Importers buy in lots, rather than buying individual rugs, so occasionally pieces are encountered that do not meet the wholesale standard of quality. Many of these rugs find their way to the auction block. Not all rugs sold at auctions are "inferior;" a few good rugs are often deliberately interspersed among the others.

Traveling auctions are announced in local newspapers with catch phrases such as "Urgent Public Auction," "To Satisfy Bank Demand," "Federal Collection Agency," or "Mandate to Liquidate." These phrases mean nothing and can be misleading. For example, "Federal" might lead you to believe that it is the government, rather than a private company, that is holding the auction.

Auction Houses. Established international auction houses have their reputation to maintain, as well as higher levels of costs to recoup. The potential buyer bids against other bidders as well as against the house. The present owner of the rug to be sold usually has a reserve placed on it, and if the bidding does not reach the desired amount, the rug is withdrawn. In several instances owners have been known to attend the auction to try to raise the bids on their own rugs.

Specialized collections and superior pieces are more likely to be offered by established auction houses because of their expertise, reputation, and ability to obtain the best possible prices for the owners. The prices obtained at these auctions will tend to reflect the actual worth of the rugs, and bargains should not be expected.

As at any auction, knowledge is a prerequisite. Ability to evaluate the condition of a rug and familiarity with current prices and auction procedures are essential. As a prospective buyer you must be able to make a realistic appraisal of what the rug may be worth on the market, as well as setting and observing a limit on what the rug is worth to you.

Estate Auctions. In an estate auction, the entire furnishings of a specific household are liquidated. Unlike the auctioneer at a traveling auction, the auctioneer has been commissioned to dispose of all items, getting the most revenue possible. As a result, the potential buyer has a chance of obtaining a rug for less than its value.

Yet risks are also present. At some estate sales, Oriental rugs are brought in to entice greater attendance. These rugs are usually from the stock of local Oriental rug or antique dealers and are being sold at a preestablished minimum. Unlike the traveling auction, where the bidding is against the house, in the estate auction potential buyers bid against each other, driving up the price. Rug dealers and other knowledgeable people are more apt to attend estate auctions, so competition can be fierce.

PURCHASING OVERSEAS It can be exciting and a lot of fun to buy an Oriental rug overseas in the local bazaar. Unfortunately, a buyer is at the mercy of the rug seller and there is little or no recourse if the merchandise is misrepresented. If you are planning a trip, it is helpful to learn beforehand about the rugs from the country and areas that you will be visiting.

Far too often, tourists who think they are getting the buy of a lifetime could have purchased the same rug at home for much less. The "silk" rug they bought turns out to be a wool rug that has been given a luster wash, or the "antique" rug has been given a wash to make it appear old. In many cases the rug you settled on may not be the one that is actually shipped home to you; a rug of much lesser quality may be substituted.

Keep in mind that the prices at your local Oriental rug retailer already include freight charges, duty, and any applicable taxes. If you buy on your own overseas, you will be liable for all of these items in addition to your purchase price. In some instances the taxes and freight charges may amount to as much as, or even more than, the price of the rug.

Trade agreements and duty charges vary from country to country, and are subject to change. Check with the proper governmental authorities about the duty or taxes imposed on Oriental rugs. Also verify the required documentation on rugs purchased as antique, and whether there are restrictions on antique rugs leaving a country.

Bargains can be found if you are willing to look for them. Before buying, check the prices in several shops, because prices can vary greatly within the same bazaar. In many places you will be expected to bargain over the price (see page 212). Do not be pressured into paying more. If possible, take your purchase home with you on the airplane. Rugs can be baled into incredibly small packages. Your rug might have a few wrinkles when you first unpack it, but these will eventually come out.

Some countries have government-operated handicraft stores. The prices here may be slightly higher than in the local bazaar, but you can generally be assured that the merchandise is as it is represented.

GOING-OUT-OF-BUSINESS SALES Going-out-of-business sales have become the newest gimmick in selling Oriental rugs to the unsuspecting public. Companies open stores on a short-lease basis with intent to "go out of business." Ads are placed in local papers and on the radio with catch phrases such as "Lease Expires," "Selling Out," "Last Days," or "Final Week." Those final weeks may go on for several years, unless there are laws to protect the consumer against deceptive advertising.

Rugs are tagged with greatly overinflated prices. Sale tags are marked "50% to 75% Reduction." Even at these so-called reductions, the marked-down price is still higher than the same rug would bring elsewhere.

The rugs being sold at these sales are often misrepresented and defective. Persian-design rugs made in India, Pakistan, and China are sold as genuine Persian rugs, at Persian rug prices; luster-washed wool rugs are sold as genuine silk rugs. All sales are final, so there is no recourse if you find that the rug purchased is not authentic, or has an objectionable flaw or repair. Wholesalers often consign their rejects to this type of sale. Many of the rugs are of poor quality with problems. For example, the rug may not lie flat on the floor, or may have a patch, repaired area, or color damage.

Appraisals and "certificates of authenticity" given with the purchase are not automatically accepted by insurance companies. If an inflated value is suspected, the appraisal is worth no more than the paper upon which it is printed. If there is an insurance claim because of a damage or loss, an independent evaluation will be made. The insurance claim will be paid on the actual value of the rug.

As the store really is not going out of business, the inventory is constantly being replaced and there is no pressure on the part of the seller to reduce prices. The rugs not sold will simply be moved to the next location, for another "going-out-of-business sale."

COMPARING SOURCES

The following criteria should help the prospective purchaser evaluate various rug sources.

Is the price fair? Comparison-shop. Prices can vary from dealer to dealer for rugs of the same type (Chinese rugs of the 90-line quality, for example), same age, and same size. Since sizes vary also, it is helpful to compute the cost per square foot or per square meter of each rug.

Can the rug be examined thoroughly? At auctions or house sales, prospective buyers often are forced to make a hasty decision without a careful inspection. Objectionable flaws or damage, such as stains, moth damage, holes, cuts in the foundation, or crooked edges, may go unnoticed at a brief first glance.

Can the rug be returned? A rug should always be taken home on approval—a standard practice among most reputable Oriental rug dealers. Ask if the rug can be returned for a full refund and not just a credit if it does not have the look desired when placed in your home or office.

Does the seller guarantee the rug? Traveling auctions may only be in town for a few days. The buyer has no recourse if the rug purchased is misrepresented or has serious or objectionable flaws. The same is true at house sales, where the rug is sold "as is" and the seller assumes no responsibility.

Never be in such a hurry to buy an Oriental rug that you fail to carefully inspect it and evaluate its merits. A few extra minutes may save a lot of time, aggravation, and money, if it is later found that costly repairs are needed.

BARGAINING

It is customary when buying an Oriental rug to make an offer lower than the stipulated or asking price, in much the same way as buying a house or a car. Bargaining is a process involving compromise, and in bargaining, knowledge is power. The final negotiating price can be strongly influenced by the knowledge of the buyer or seller.

Bargaining may be appropriate almost any time you are trying to buy an Oriental rug, whether from an individual or from a rug merchant. The merchant has already incurred certain costs related to the rug and their prices tend to reflect current market conditions; therefore, their ability and willingness to bargain are somewhat restricted. An individual, on the other hand, may have set the price arbitrarily through a lack of market information and have only a minimal investment in the rug, which may have been inherited or held for some time.

In any bargaining situation, knowledge makes the position of the buyer more certain and strategically sound. The better informed you are, the more likely the compromise will be in your favor.

EVALUATING RUG CONDITION

The carpet as a whole must be considered before making a detailed investigation of its component parts. If the colors are pleasing and the pattern well executed, then the potential buyer should check the carpet's structure.

Each of the following points discussed does affect the value of the rug, and the price should reflect its overall condition. A small flaw that might be objectionable to one person is not always objectionable to another. Since Oriental rugs are individually handcrafted, minor flaws will usually be found; absolute perfection should not be expected. If a rug has a deficiency, it is important that the purchaser be aware of the flaw and how it affects the rug's value; such information is necessary for an informed decision.

OVERALL EXAMINATION The carpet should lie flat on the floor. Wrinkles or ridges are caused by improper warp tension and will not come out. These areas will wear rapidly as well as appear unsightly. Creases caused by the rug's being folded or a slight rippling of the selvedge, however, will work their way out over a period of time.

Holes or breaks in the foundation become very visible when the back of the rug is held up to the light. Patches and rewoven areas also are easier to see on the back of the rug. It is advisable to get an estimate for the repair if the rug is being sold "as is."

Worn spots and wear areas are objectionable in an old Oriental rug. It is preferable to have an old rug that is evenly worn.

Slight irregularities in the rug's sides and ends are to be expected in village and tribal rugs; however, crooked ends and sides are objectionable in finely woven city pieces. Minor irregularities can be corrected by having the rug sized or stretched. This process should be done by the rug dealer before the rug is purchased. The rug should be carefully inspected afterward to ensure that the irregularities have been satisfactorily removed.

Each rug should be carefully inspected to make certain that no borders or portions of borders have been removed, especially at the fringed ends of the rug. The rug should have the same border arrangement on all four sides and should not have been cut or shortened in any way. Turkoman rugs and Turkoman-design rugs from India and Pakistan are the exception, since they characteristically have dissimilar sides and borders. Some Chinese and Tibetan rugs have no border arrangement.

The types of dyes used should be given careful consideration because of their effect on

---

CHECKLIST FOR EVALUATING A RUG'S CONDITION

PILE
  Low areas
  Moth damage
  Painted
  Faded
  Color run

WARP AND WEFT THREADS
  Breaks when bent or folded
  Supple and flexible

FRINGE
  Original or added

SELVEDGE
  Original or added

KNOTS
  Rows of knots missing from ends
  Rows of knots missing from sides

BACK
  Holes
  Patches or repaired areas

---

fading and running. Have the colors faded or will they run when the rug is washed? Wiping a damp cloth over the top of a rug is a good test to determine if the dyes are colorfast. If there are traces of dye on the cloth, that color is not fixed. This can be corrected and should be done only by an Oriental rug professional.

A rug in which the dyes have already run should be obvious by the blurred design. This is especially visible on the white or light-colored areas of the rug. By comparing the colors on the front and back of the rug, you can tell whether or not the rug has faded. The back of a faded rug will be much darker than the sunlight-faded front. Aniline dyes will have produced all of these undesirable effects (see page 28).

STRUCTURE Examining the structure of any rug is important; for a used rug, it is essential. A used rug has had more opportunities to be mistreated or improperly cared for. Many of the results of improper treatment are not immediately apparent on casual inspection.

Pile. The pile should be checked for worn areas, holes, and moth damage. Moth damage may appear on the top of the rug, the pile having been eaten down to the foundation; or it may be hidden on the back of the rug. The portion of the knot that is looped around the warp thread may also have been eaten. When this occurs, there is nothing securing the pile to the foundation of the rug and you can easily remove a tuft of pile by pulling.

If the pile is well worn, the knots themselves are visible. This may occur in spots, rather than uniformly over the surface of the rug, as when caused by heavy traffic. In the event that the pile is worn to the foundation, a check should be made to see if the warp and weft threads have been painted to cover up the wear areas.

In the pile of older rugs, white knots are sometimes visible. These are knots in the warp or weft threads. All rugs have them, but they are more noticeable in older rugs with a low pile. If these knots are objectionable to you, they can easily be touched up with any colorfast dye.

If dead or skin wool (see page 21) has been used for the pile, the fibers will be brittle and will not wear well. In a used rug, worn spots caused by the dead wool will be quite obvious. In a new rug, dead wool can be felt by running one's hand across the pile; the dead wool has a definite coarse, bristly feel.

Warp and weft threads should be checked for cuts and breaks. The rug should be turned completely over to facilitate inspection. Cuts or breaks in the warp and weft threads can become serious if not repaired before the rug is purchased.

Fringe. An inspection of the fringe should be made to determine if it is the original or if a new fringe has been added. Folding a rug back at the end of the pile is the easiest way to check whether the fringe is an unbroken extension of the warp threads. A refringed rug will have warp threads that terminate (either by being cut or turned under) and an attached fringed band. A rug that has been cut and had new fringe added is less valuable than a rug with its original fringe, even if the original fringe is not in particularly good condition.

Selvedges bind the sides (terminal warp threads) of the carpet. They do not wear as quickly as the fringe but do on occasion need to be reovercast. The reovercasting should always be done by hand rather than machine.

Knots. The *jufti*, or "false" knot, has been used in some Persian and Indian rugs (see page 22). It is a knot tied around four warp threads instead of the usual two. A rug woven with the jufti knot has half the number of knots and the pile is half as dense; consequently, these rugs are much less resistant to wear.

ORIENTAL-DESIGN RUGS

Rugs with Oriental designs are widely available. They are made in numerous countries throughout the world and are sold under a variety of brand names. Oriental-design rugs can be made with wool, cotton, jute, or viscose, polypropylene, and other synthetic fibers. Their designs have been copied from Persian, Turkish, Chinese, Caucasian, and Turkoman carpets.

Oriental-design rugs are machine made and should not be confused with the hand-knotted or handwoven genuine Oriental rugs. An Oriental rug *must* be handmade, either hand-knotted or handwoven. An Oriental-design rug will depreciate with use and will not maintain its value. Yet the price of a good-quality, wool Oriental-design rug can be as much as, and sometimes more than, a genuine Oriental rug. Oriental-design rugs manufactured in North America and Europe have much higher production costs than rugs woven in China and the Middle East.

Four elements of carpet construction serve as checkpoints in determining whether a rug is a genuine Oriental or a machine-made imitation. These are the back, fringed ends, sides, and knots. It is necessary to check all four elements before making a final evaluation.

There are several different types of backing found on Oriental-design rugs. On the *back* of a machine-made rug, the design is often not as crisp and clear with the hand-knotted rug. Some Oriental-design rugs made in Hong Kong and Korea have a canvas backing; others may have a backing of jute. On the back of a hand-knotted rug, the design is clear unless multiple or thick wefts are used. The appearance of carpet backs varies according to where they were woven.

By folding a genuine Oriental rug and spreading the pile, you can see loops of yarn surrounding the warp threads. The pile of a machine-made rug, on the other hand, has been

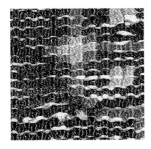 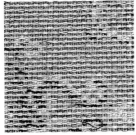  

| BACK OF HAND-KNOTTED RUG | BACK OF A MACHINE-MADE RUG | PILE OF A HAND-MADE RUG | PILE OF A MACHINE-MADE RUG |

KNOTTED FRINGE OF A
HAND-MADE RUG

MACHINE-MADE FRINGE
ATTACHED DURING
MANUFACTURING

MACHINE-MADE FRINGE
ADDED TO A RUG

attached by being stitched, glued, or looped under a single warp thread.

The *fringed ends* and sides of a rug offer other points for comparison. The fringe of a genuine Oriental rug is an extension of the carpet's warp threads; the manner in which the fringes are finished varies from one weaving center to another. Machine-made rugs, in contrast, may have a fringe composed of cotton strands that have been overcast or sewn onto the ends of the carpet, or a fringe that has been made separately and then attached. This type of fringe is sometimes added to Oriental rugs to replace the worn original fringe.

The *sides* of a genuine Oriental rug are weft-wrapped or overcast in wool, cotton, silk, or goat's hair. The material used for the overcasting varies depending on the weaving center. The majority of machine-made rugs have sides that have been bound with a machine serging; the sides of some, however, have been left with a natural selvedge. Old and antique Oriental rugs are occasionally found with sides that have been machine serged.

KNOT COUNT

One of the first questions a prospective Oriental rug buyer often asks is, "How many knots per square inch?" Many buyers are lured into a false sense of security by believing that the higher the knot count, the better, the more valuable, and the more desirable the rug. Knot count is only *one* indicator used in determining the quality and value of an Oriental rug.

Knot count is a feature basic to the construction of all Oriental rugs. It simply measures the tightness of the weave and the number of knots in a given area. Knot count is quoted in knots per square inch or per square meter. (See the opposite page for conversion formulas.) The number of knots per square inch can vary greatly. Knot count is calculated by counting the number of loops (knot backs) that fall within a 1-inch (or 1-decimeter) square. Lay a ruler along a weft thread on the back of the rug and count the number of knots in an inch (decimeter); repeat the process vertically. (When knots are tied on warp threads on the same level, each knot will have two loops clearly visible.) Multiplying the two numbers together gives the number of knots

MEASUREMENT CONVERSION FORMULAS			
WHEN YOU HAVE	TO FIND		
centimeters	feet	divide by	30.48
centimeters	inches	divide by	2.54
feet	centimeters	multiply by	30.48
inches	centimeters	multiply by	2.54
square feet	square meters	multiply by	0.09
square meters	square feet	divide by	10.76
square yards	square meters	multiply by	1.20
square meters	square yards	divide by	8.36

per square inch (decimeter). This should be done in five different areas scattered over the back of the rug, and those results averaged.

Although it is generally true that a higher knot count indicates a more desirable rug, there are too many factors involved for this assumption always to be accurate. The age, condition, rarity, and country of origin of the rug must be taken into account as well. Thus an antique Khotan rug from Xinjiang , China will be more valuable than an Indian carpet of the same knot count, age, and condition, simply because Khotan rugs are scarcer. Knot count should be used only when comparing rugs from the same weaving center, in the same condition, and of the same age. Each rug possesses its own attributes and is unique unto itself, further complicating comparisons between rugs.

Some countries have a different way of denoting the quality of their Oriental rugs. In China, the term used is "line" (for example, 90-line), a designation that can be converted to the more common number of knots per square inch. The "line" number is the number of pairs of warp threads per linear foot, which in turn is the same as the number of knots per linear foot. A 90-line rug has 90 knots per linear foot, both horizontally and vertically, which is equivalent to

WOOL OVERCASTING
ON THE SIDE OF A
HAND-MADE
YAGCIBEDIR RUG

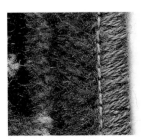

YARN SERGING
ON THE SIDE
OF A MACHINE-
MADE RUG

SELVEDGE
OF A
MACHINE-MADE
RUG

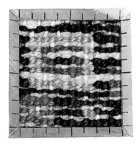

COUNTING
THE KNOTS
PER SQUARE
INCH

approximately 56 knots per square inch ($90 \div 12 \times 90 \div 12 = 56$). Each weaving center has its own characteristic range of knot counts (see pages 234 to 237). Individual rugs from the same weaving center, however, do vary in knot count. Rugs with higher knot counts have a denser pile than those with lower knot counts. A dense pile leads to a sturdier, more durable rug. The pile of a high-knot-count rug is usually cut shorter, yielding a crisp design. These rugs are relatively more expensive than those with lower knot counts.

DECORATING WITH ORIENTAL RUGS

There are two ways to focus when decorating with or around an Oriental rug: first, if you have a definite area that needs to be covered, and second, if you like a particular rug and must find the perfect place to display it. The ideal way to decorate with an Oriental rug is to start with the rug and work upward to the upholstery, drapes, and wall color. In reality, however, few of us can afford to start from scratch and redo an entire room at one time. If you are buying a rug for a specific area, make sure that you can take the rug home on approval to see how it will blend with or highlight the existing decor.

When shopping for your Oriental carpet, it is helpful to make a few notes to take with you about the desired size, color scheme, and design preference. It is also helpful to take swatches of upholstery fabric and color samples if you have them. Paint samples are an excellent source for colors you may be trying to match.

Considering the area to be covered is the first step. Establish acceptable minimum and maximum areas and look only at rugs that fall within this range. Do not fall in love with a rug that is too large or small. An Oriental carpet should complement and enhance the feeling of a room, not dominate it; nor should a rug be too small, looking like a postage stamp in a huge area.

If an Oriental rug is to be used under a dining room table, it should be wide enough so the chairs can be moved freely without catching their back legs on the rug. Conversation areas in living rooms or family rooms can be defined with an Oriental rug. Large open-area room plans can be separated into living and dining areas with the use of rugs. When using an Oriental rug in a long passage or hall, the runner should not stop in the middle of a doorway.

Lighting used in stores often is very different from what you have at home and the overall color tones may give a different impression. Some rugs with deep rich colors seem to absorb light. These rugs should be placed in a room with a lot of natural light. For rooms with very little natural light, choose a rug with a lighter color palette that reflects light.

In addition, most rugs have a light side and a dark side. This is especially visible in Pakistani and Chinese rugs. Be sure to turn the rug to see which side gives the desired effect.

The popularity of color combinations used in Oriental carpets is constantly changing. Limitless color combinations can be found, from strong primary colors to soft pastel shades. It is not necessary that every color in the rug match exactly the colors in the fabrics in the room; however, they should blend and yield a harmonious effect.

A central medallion rug goes well under a dining room table with legs, but a table with a pedestal base will obscure a medallion. A living room arrangement may look unbalanced if a medallion is not centered in the room. An alternative would be an overall or a repeated-pattern rug. A one-directional rug should be placed so that the full impact of the design is seen. The Vase or Tree-of-Life pattern should be viewed when entering a room, rather than from the far end. Small rugs with a one-directional pattern, such as prayer rugs, make excellent wall hangings.

When decorating with antique rugs, make certain that the upholstered-furniture fabric in the room does not make the rug look shabby. New and antique rugs usually do not mix well together; one may make the other look bad. This is true because of the colors found in both types: the more mellow tones of an antique rug can make a modern rug look very harsh in comparison.

Saddle and storage bags can be stuffed and used as cushions or pillows to accentuate a sofa or fireplace hearth. In addition to bags, fragments and pieces of old, worn-out, and damaged Oriental rugs can be used to make pillows and cushions. Large pieces or fragments of Oriental rugs can be used to upholster a stool or a chair.

Kelims make excellent fabric from which to upholster cushions, stools, or chairs. They are flexible and easy to work with and the results can be very dramatic. Turkish kelims often are woven in two strips which can be separated and used as drapes.

If you have a rug that you want to be the center of focus, place it over a mantel, above a buffet, or in a stairwell. Small silk prayer rugs make excellent wall hangings. Large rugs can be placed in the center of a conversation area or under a glass-top table.

HANGING AN ORIENTAL RUG

Oriental rugs make excellent wall hangings if you have a large expanse of wall area to be covered. Long Oriental rug runners, for example, can make a dramatic effect when hung in a stairwell. In addition to the esthetic value, Oriental rugs provide insulation and absorb sound.

There are several different methods that can be used for hanging rugs:

- The rug can be nailed directly on the wall. Small nails can be worked carefully through the carpet without damaging it. The nails should be placed every 2 to 3 inches to distribute the weight of the rug equally. This method works well for rugs of any size.
- Rugs can be suspended from a "tack strip," a strip of wood with nails used for installing wall-to-wall carpets. The tack strip is attached directly to the wall and the small nails grip the carpet to be hung. Large and heavy rugs may need several rows of tack strip.
- Another method is to sew loops or a casing along the back of the rug, then insert a metal rod through the loops or casing. This rod can in turn be attached to the wall by a pair of brackets.
- Velcro can also be used to hang an Oriental rug. A band of Velcro three to four inches in width should be used. One side of the Velcro band is sewn to the back of the rug and the other side is attached either directly to the wall or to a board, which is in turn attached to the wall.

REPAIRING A KELIM IN PESHAWAR, PAKISTAN

sixteen

RUG CARE AND REPAIR

An Oriental rug requires very little care. They are extremely durable and withstand wear and traffic better than machine-made carpeting. There are a few things that can be done to prolong the life and beauty of the rug, such as routine vacuuming and cleaning.

RUG CARE

There are opposing views as to how often one should clean and vacuum a rug. In the countries where Oriental rugs are made, it is customary to remove one's shoes upon entering the home. In the West, shoes are commonly worn indoors. The outdoor dirt and grit they bring in can eventually grind its way into the body of the carpet, making it necessary to vacuum more often. Vacuuming once a week is usually sufficient for a carpet under normal conditions.

Avoid putting plant pots on a rug, even if they have a waterproof liner. Extra moisture will build up under the pot and the consequent mildew and rot will permanently damage the rug, depreciating its value.

Any Oriental rug that is in a high-traffic area should be rotated periodically to allow for even wear. Every six months to a year is recommended.

UNDERPADS Though Oriental rugs have the remarkable ability to withstand wear, their life span is doubled with the use of a good-quality underpad. Numerous types of underpadding in various thicknesses are available: hair or fiber filled with rubberized surfaces, rubber with jute surface, or foam.

An Oriental rug placed over broadloom will wrinkle and move. The amount of movement depends on the type of broadloom. There are special underpads designed to prevent a rug from moving which work with varying degrees of success. The most successful is a relatively thin fabric with adhesive properties on both sides. Once the pad is in place the rug will remain firm, but the adhesive properties are lost if the rug is routinely moved. Another pad, a thin, rather fuzzy foam, is not as effective as the adhesive type. Least successful of all is a plastic grid with small spikes that attaches to the Oriental rug.

VACUUMING Oriental rugs should be vacuumed regularly. Care should be taken not to catch the carpet end or fringe in the vacuum cleaner. If this happens, one's first reaction is to quickly pull the carpet or fringe out of the machine, but this will put a strain on the fringe and cause it to break. Instead, immediately turn off the vacuum; the fringe can then be easily removed.

Ideally, the vacuuming should be done in the same direction as the nap of the carpet or across the carpet. It should not be done against the grain—especially when vacuuming silk carpets. Vacuuming in the wrong direction will result in ridges in the silk pile.

CLEANING An Oriental rug should be washed or cleaned when it becomes soiled or dirty. The frequency of cleaning depends on the use and the color of the rug.

It is advisable to have your rug cleaned by a reputable firm that specializes in the cleaning of Oriental rugs. Rugs should be washed with a neutral soap and thoroughly rinsed. The thorough rinsing is important to remove any soap residue in the pile. Soil and dirt will adhere to soap-covered fibers, causing the rug to have a dull appearance and a slightly sticky feel, and it will resoil quickly.

A thorough cleaning may not be advisable if there is a risk of color run. In this case a surface cleaning is preferable, even if it does not remove all the embedded soil and grit. At least it will prevent the colors from running.

Before a really dirty carpet is washed, it should be turned upside down and its back lightly tapped or vacuumed, to loosen the ground-in dirt and grit from the base of the pile. Then turn the carpet over and vacuum the pile. This process may need to be repeated several times.

If you want to clean a small rug at home, place the rug on a patio or driveway and thoroughly wet it. Add a small amount of neutral soap and brush the pile with a soft-bristle brush in the same direction as the pile. After the entire surface has been washed, rinse and dry the rug thoroughly. Remember that it is the water that moves the soil, not the soap. Soap helps break down the surface tension, which enables the water to penetrate the fiber. Water flushes the soil out of the pile.

STORAGE Before storing any rug, it should be thoroughly cleaned, dried, and preferably mothproofed. Insects and rodents are attracted to dirty carpets, especially to urine stains or any food crumbs which may be left on the carpet.

Rugs should be stored in a dry area that is not subject to extreme changes in temperature and humidity. Unfinished attics and basements are not good places for storing rugs. Attics can harbor mice, rats, and squirrels, which may find the Oriental rug an ideal nesting place. A stored rug is also an ideal target for moths, which are attracted to dark, undisturbed areas. Basements often have high humidity and are subject to flooding. High humidity causes mildew, mold, and rot.

The rug should be rolled, not folded, in the direction of the pile and wrapped in heavy paper, preferably acid-free, or cloth. Plastic wrapping should be used only for storing rugs for short periods of time. The rug must be completely dry as any moisture can cause it to mildew. If the rug is to be stored for a long period of time, it is advisable to unroll it from time to time to check it for humidity or insects.

If you need to store a very large rug, it may need to be folded and loosely rolled. Be careful not to strain or break the foundation. A thick-bodied rug, such as a Bijar, should be rolled with the pile side out. Creases caused by folding are temporary, and will eventually come out after the rug is relaid.

MOTHS Moths can be a major problem with an Oriental rug. If you have seen moths in your home, your rugs should be mothproofed. They should be vacuumed regularly, especially the parts that are under furniture. Moths are attracted to dark, undisturbed areas. Rugs hung on the wall are also subject to moth attacks and should be taken down from time to time and thoroughly vacuumed both front and back.

If you have seen moths, it is very important to eliminate the source of the infestation. Once this source has been removed, eliminating the moths is not difficult. You can find moth infestation in the stuffing of old chairs, ottomans, or woolen clothes. Check in closets and old chests for woolen items which may have been stored for a long time.

A rug that is infested with moths must be treated immediately. Moth eggs look and feel like salt. The live moths can be killed easily either with an insecticide or by vacuuming the front and back of the rug, then washing and rinsing it thoroughly to remove any traces of larvae and eggs. The carpet then should be mothproofed. Mothproofing an infested rug does not by itself kill the eggs or larvae.

REPAIRS

During the lifetime of a rug, repairs may be necessary. Prompt attention should be taken before a minor problem develops into a major repair. Minor repairs can be done at home and are fun to do if you like needlework; however, major repairs should be undertaken by a professional.

There are three types of repairs that can be done: restoration, conservation, and utilitarian. *Restoration* means returning the rug to its original state, and includes reweaving a damaged area or replacing fringe and side finishes. *Conservation* keeps the rug in its present condition and secures fragile areas so that no further deterioration will occur. This involves taking appropriate measures to protect any eroding areas, such as a hole, the ends, or sides. *Utilitarian* repair makes the rug usable, such as patching a hole in an old and tattered rug that cannot be restored to its original condition. Not every old rug is valuable. Even a rug with sentimental value, and no monetary value, has its dollar limits when you are contemplating a repair.

Before having a rug repaired, discuss the type of repair to be done and how the work is to be accomplished. As there are usually several different methods to be undertaken, decide which is the best for the rug. If the cost of the repair is more than you want to spend at the present time, ask if some conservation measures can be done until you want to undertake complete restoration.

Any breaks or cracks in the foundation, warp, or weft threads of a carpet should be attended to at once, before the pile becomes loosened. Foundation breaks often occur because of dry rot or moisture from a plant container.

REWEAVING Reweaving should be undertaken by a professional. A good repair should not be readily visible. Reweaving can be expensive and only be done if the value of the rug justifies the expense. If the pile has been only slightly damaged—such as by moth damage, burns, or wear lines—the warp and wefts often are intact. It is then only necessary to have the damaged area reknotted and trimmed the same length as the rest of the pile.

An alternative to reknotting the pile is a "flat stitch," which can be used to cover worn areas when the pile of the rug is worn to the base of the knots. If the pile is not worn, reknotting will be necessary. The flat stitch is successful on Caucasian, Herez, and Hamadan rugs when they are worn to the base of the knots, and is less expensive than reknotting.

If the rug has a hole, new warp and weft threads must be inserted before reweaving can take place. A frame must be built and the carpet attached. This is done in order to maintain an even warp tension. Once the new warps are inserted, the knots are tied and the wefts replaced. This type of repair requires considerable skill and is difficult to do invisibly. It is best left to a professional.

PATCHING If the damaged portion of the rug is too extensive to consider reweaving or the value of the rug does not justify the cost, patching is the best alternative. A fragment or portion of another rug of similar design can be inserted into the damaged area and secured. Sometimes the patch is reinforced by glue or a lining on the back. This type of repair can make the rug usable and is inexpensive.

FRINGES The fringe of a carpet is extremely vulnerable and is often the first area to need attention and repair. Fringes can get caught in the vacuum cleaner or be eaten by animals, and because they are so thin, are subjected to the most strenuous wear. Unless the ends of the rug are secured, knot loss will occur. To ensure against such an outcome, an overcasting or blanket stitch can be done by hand along a straight weft thread, using buttonhole or carpet thread. This securing of the weft thread will in turn hold the rows of knots in place and prevent pile loss.

SECURING THE FRINGED
END OF A RUG

If the fringe has been worn to the kelim end, the wefts can be removed, leaving the exposed warps to form a short natural fringe. If the rug is worn into the pile, and knot loss has already occurred and part of the carpet has been worn unevenly away, the uneven portion can be pulled back to the first continuous weft. Overcasting with the blanket stitch will secure the end of the rug from further knot loss.

Fringe can be replaced by reinserting warp threads into the body of the rug. This process is expensive and should be done only if the value of the rug justifies the expense.

SIDES The sides of a carpet are not as susceptible to wear as the fringe; however, the wool overcasting may need to be replaced eventually. Replacing the wool overcasting is the simplest and easiest of side repairs. If the side consists of a single cord that is wrapped with wool, a yarn as close in color to the original should be used and wrapped around the cord.

OVERCASTING WITH WOOL
THE WORN SIDES OF A RUG

Some rugs require only that the overcast cord on the side be reattached. Pakistani rugs often require this type of repair. The side cords are not weft-wrapped during the weaving process but are added once the carpet has been completed. If caught in a vacuum or pulled, the side cords tend to separate from the rug. They can be reattached with a strong thread. This should be attended to before there is knot loss.

Missing side cords should be replaced with a cord of similar diameter as the original. The cord must be attached and secured to the body of the rug before the cord can be overcast with wool.

ROLLED SIDES AND CORNERS The sides and corners of finely knotted rugs have a tendency to turn under and roll. This is caused by tight beating and pulling of the weft threads.

A leather or vinyl strip about 2 inches wide should be sewn to the back of the rug. This strip should be sewn just inside the selvedge with a broad cross-stitch across the strip, using a heavy carpet or buttonhole thread.

STAIN REMOVAL

Spills should be immediately blotted with a paper towel. Any remaining stain should be diluted with water and blotted up again. This process should be repeated until the stain is gone. Lightly wipe the carpet in the same direction as the pile. Be sure to remove all the excess water put onto the soiled area. The affected area should be lifted to allow complete drying.

Never rub the area because this causes the spill to be more readily absorbed into the fibers. It also causes an unsightly pile disturbance that cannot be corrected. Never apply household bleach or vinegar to a spot or stain. Vinegar contains acetic acid, which will permanently fix the stain.

Professional stain removal can be an expensive process, depending on the type and size of stain as well as the type of carpet involved. Removing stains is a slow process since various bleaching agents are applied and allowed to dry and the process repeated until the stain is removed.

Unfortunately, some stains are permanent. They may be lightened to some degree, but some residue will remain. If a trace of stain is unacceptable, reweaving the area is an alternative.

GLOSSARY OF RUG TERMS

ABRASH. A color variation or stripe of a slightly different hue across the body of a carpet, the result of a slight color difference in the dye lots used.

ALLOVER DESIGN. A rug field pattern that instead of a repeated or regimented form has large-scale patterns filling the field.

ANATOLIAN. Name loosely applied to all Turkish rugs from the Anatolian plateau.

ANILINE DYE. A synthetic dye derived from benzol, a product of coal tar, introduced to the carpet industry in the third quarter of the 19th century. The dyes were not colorfast and faded when exposed to sunlight.

ANTIQUE FINISH. A chemical wash used to tone down colors and give a rug an old or antique appearance.

ARA-KHACHI. Turkish term for the middle or main border of a carpet. *See* Bala-khachi.

AUBUSSON. A pileless (flat-weave) rug, generally with a floral medallion in pastel colors, once woven in France. The designs of these rugs have been adapted to pile carpets and are now woven in India and China.

AY GUL. A moon-shaped motif used as the medallion in rugs from Eastern Turkestan.

BAFF. Persian word for knot.

BALA-KHACHI. Turkish term for the small border stripe on either side of a carpet's main border. *See* Ara-khachi.

BERDELIK. Rug used as a wall hanging. Silk rugs generally fit into this category.

BID MAJNUN. Weeping Willow rug design, or a combination of weeping willow, cyprus, and poplar tree motifs.

BORDER. A band or series of bands surrounding the field and focal point of a carpet.

BOTEH. A small Oriental rug motif that resembles a pinecone or pear.

BROCADE. A weaving technique whereby a supplementary weft is added into the ground weft to create a pattern.

BUKHARA. Name associated with Turkoman-design rugs woven in India and Pakistan. Also an ancient marketplace for the rugs of Turkestan.

CARDING. Process for preparing wool for spinning, in which two wooden paddles with metal teeth entangle the fibers so that they lie in different directions, yielding a soft, fuzzy wool.

CARTOON. A piece of graph or squared paper on which a rug pattern has been drawn, used as a guide in weaving. Each square represents a single knot, the color of which is keyed to the color of the square. *See* Talim.

CARTOUCHE. A cloudlike motif that often surrounds a date or an inscription woven in a rug.

CARVED PILE. Grooves cut into the rug pile to accentuate the borders and designs, done in some Chinese and Indian carpets.

CAUCASIAN. Refers to rugs woven in the Caucasus Mountain region, a narrow strip of land between the Black and Caspian seas. The rugs are brightly colored and have highly stylized designs.

CEYREK. Turkish term for small rugs, measuring approximately 2 feet 9 inches by 4 feet 6 inches (90 by 140 centimeters).

CHROME DYE. A colorfast synthetic dye developed in the 20th century and used in the dyeing of wool.

CHURDJUN. A small saddlebag. Also spelled as Khorjin.

CHUVAL (TCHUVAL). A large storage bag usually hung from the interior framework of the Turkoman yurt, or tent dwelling.

CICIM. A type of weft-float pileless weave, in which an additional colored weft is interlaced into a rug's regular warp and weft system, giving the appearance of solid lines over the ground weave.

CLOSED-BACK. Term referring to the appearance of the back of a Chinese carpet. The weft threads of a closed-back carpet are not visible when the carpet is observed from the back, since the knots completely cover them.

COCHINEAL. Red dye derived from the dried bodies of a species of insect (*Dactylopius coccus cacti*).

COLORFAST. Term used for a rug dye that does not change color when subjected to washing or exposed to sunlight.

COLOR RUN. Term for the bleeding of one color in a rug onto an adjacent color.

COMBING. Process for preparing wool for spinning, in which wool fibers are pulled through a wooden comb with metal teeth, aligning the fibers in the same direction.

CORROSION. Deterioration of dyed fiber because of the oxidation of a mordant containing particles of iron, often seen in dark-brown or black wool.

CUT-LOOP TECHNIQUE. Tibetan method of weaving carpets. A strand of yarn is looped around pairs of warp threads and then around a rod; after a row is completed a knife is run along the rod, cutting the pile.

DASTGAH. Persian word for *loom*.

DHURRIE. A pileless carpet, usually woven in India with either cotton or wool. The design is created by interweaving colored weft threads through the warp threads.

DOBAG. Acronym for a weaving project in Turkey administered by Marmara University in Istanbul to reestablish the use of natural dyes and to standardize the quality grades of rugs.

DOZAR. Persian term for rugs measuring 4 feet 6 inches by 7 feet (135 by 210 centimeters) in size.

ELEM. *See* Skirt.

EMBROIDERY. Decoration done with a needle after the rug has been woven.

EMBOSSED PILE. Sculptured rug pile, or pile that has been woven longer than the rest of the ground and then trimmed to give a relief effect.

ENSI. A pile or flat weave rug used to cover the doorway of a Turkoman tent.

FLAT WEAVE. Term used to describe any pileless weaving, such as Jajim, Kelim, or Soumak.

FLOAT. The portion of a warp or weft thread that passes over and under two more warp or weft threads.

FOUNDATION. Collective term referring to both the warp and weft threads of a carpet.

FRINGE. The loose ends of a carpet's warp threads emerging from the upper and lower ends of the carpet. It may be either knotted or plain.

FUGITIVE DYE. Any dye that fades with time.

GALI. Persian term for the main carpet in the traditional Persian arrangement. *See* Kellei.

GHIORDES KNOT. Symmetrical or Turkish knot used in rug weaving, in which a strand of wool encircles both warp threads, with the loose ends drawn tightly between the two.

GIREH. Persian word for *knot*.

GUL. A small rectilinear emblem, once unique to the Turkoman tribes that used them in their rugs. Different Turkoman tribal guls have since been adopted by the weaving centers of India and Pakistan.

HALI. Turkish word for *carpet*.

HARSHANG. Persian rug pattern, similar to the Shah Abbas pattern, with large motifs that suggest a crab.

HATCHLI. Rug design, originally Turkoman, in which the field is divided into quadrants by wide bars or stripes.

Herati. Rug pattern consisting of a rosette surrounded by four leaves or "fish." The rosette is usually found inside a diamond shape (lozenge), although it need not be. *See* Mahi.

Hitch. Term used in Isfahan, Iran, to refer to the quality of a rug, 100 warp threads per hitch.

Indigo. Natural blue dye derived from the leaves of the indigo plant (*Indigo tinctoria*).

Ipekli. Turkish term for artificial silk. A blend of mercerized cotton and silk waste or rayon, it is used for the pile in some Turkish carpets.

Jajim. A warp-faced weave in which a supplementary design warp is employed as a float. The striped textiles are woven in narrow strips and sewn together.

Jufti knot. A modified symmetrical or asymmetrical rug knot in which the weaver uses four warp threads per knot instead of two, resulting in half the number of knots and half the amount of wool in a given area. Also called double knot.

Keleyghi. Persian term for a long, narrow rug measuring approximately 6 by 13 feet (1.80 by 4 meters). Also the side runners in the traditional Persian layout.

Kelim. A weft-faced weave created by interweaving colored weft threads through the warp threads. This type of weave is used for rugs, storage bags and animal covers. Also the finished terminal portion of a carpet falling between the pile and the fringes.

Kellei. Persian term for a large rectangular carpet measuring approximately 7 feet 6 inches by 18 feet (230 by 600 centimeters). Also called Gali.

Kenereh. Persian term for runners measuring approximately 2 feet 6 inches by 8 feet (75 by 245 centimeters) or 3 feet 6 inches by 20 feet (105 by 600 centimeters).

Khorjin. A small saddlebag. Also spelled as *Churdjun*.

Kiaba. Refers to a rug approximately 6 feet 6 inches by 9 feet 9 inches (2 by 3 meters) in size.

Kis (Kiz). Turkish word for girl or bride. When used in conjunction with a type of rug, it indicates a rug given as a wedding gift from the bride to the groom.

Kork wool. The finest quality of wool used in rug weaving, from the spring shearing. It consists of the underhairs from the sheep's shoulders and flanks.

Lazy lines. Diagonal lines visible in certain carpets, caused by the reversing of the weft thread back on itself rather than its being carried across the width of the carpet.

Lechek. Persian term for the corner design, or spandrel, of a rug.

Lechek torunj. Persian term for any design with corner and central medallions.

Madder. Natural red dye made from the root of the madder plant (*Rubia tinctorum*).

Mafrash. A four-sided storage bag.

Mahi. Persian wool for fish. Another term for the Herati pattern.

Mihrab. The arch or niche of a prayer rug, from the name of the niche in a mosque indicating the direction of Mecca.

Mina khani. Rug design composed of repeated floral motifs surrounded by four similar smaller flowers joined by vines to form a diamond arrangement.

Moghad. Term used in Mashad, Iran, to denote the quality of a rug, namely 12,000 knots per square meter.

Mordant. A fixative used in the dyeing of wool, which enables the dye to affix itself to the wool.

Morgi. Persian word for *hen*, and for an imaginative rug motif resembling a chicken.

Muska. Small triangular shapes, symbols of good luck, often woven into Turkish rugs.

Naqshe. Persian word for *pattern* or *design*.

Natural dye. A dye derived from a plant, root, flower, fruit, tree, insect, or shell.

Node. The loop portion of the knot as viewed from the back of the rug.

Palas. A Caucasian kelim.

Panel design. Rug design in which the field is divided into rectangular compartments, each of which encloses one or more motifs.

Patina. The sheen acquired by the pile of a rug with age and use.

Persian knot. Rug-weaving knot in which a strand of wool encircles one warp thread and winds loosely around the other. Also called asymmetrical or Senna knot.

Pile. Nap of the rug; the clipped ends of the knotted wool.

Ply. Two or more strands of yarn, either wool or cotton, that are twisted together. This process is done in the opposite direction as the yarn is spun.

Pushti. Persian term for a small pillow cover or small rug, approximately 2 by 3 feet (60 by 90 centimeters).

Radj. Term used in Tabriz, Iran, in denoting the quality of a rug. A *radj* equals 7 centimeters.

Saff. A "family" prayer rug; a design that has multiple mihrabs in a series, side by side.

Savonnerie. A rug hand-knotted in France, with a thick, heavy pile and pastel colors. New copies are now being woven in Romania.

Scoarte. Kelim woven in Romania with a slit-tapestry technique.

Sculptured pile. Embossed rug pile, or pile that has been woven longer than the rest of the ground and then trimmed to give a relief effect.

Seccades. Turkish term for carpets that measure approximately 3 feet 9 inches by 6 feet 6 inches (115 by 200 centimeters).

Sedjadeh. Persian word for a prayer carpet, or for a carpet measuring approximately 4 feet 6 inches by 7 feet (135 by 210 centimeters).

Selvedge. The side finish of a carpet; the terminal warp threads have been wrapped with the weft threads.

Senna knot. Asymmetrical or Persian rug knot; a strand of yarn encircles one warp thread and winds loosely around the other.

Shah Abbas. Allover rug design with various types of palmettes, cloudbands, and vases interconnected by some form of stalk or tendril. Named after Shah Abbas (ruled 1587–1628), patron of Persian carpet making.

Shared-warp technique. Pileless rug-weaving technique in which different-colored wefts meet and share a common warp, loop around the warp, and double back on themselves.

Shou. Chinese character symbolizing long life.

Sinekli. Turkish term for a small, flylike rug motif.

Skirt. Or **Elem**, an additional panel or band woven at the top and bottom of most Turkoman-design rugs and bags.

Slit-weave technique. Pileless rug-weaving technique in which when different-colored wefts meet, the two colors are kept separate so that each thread doubles back on itself, creating a slit at the juncture. Also know as slit tapestry.

Sofreh. A woven eating cloth, spread on the ground like a picnic cloth.

Souf. Rug weave that combines a flat weave for the background and a knotted-pile technique for the motifs, giving a relief effect to the design.

Soumak. Pileless carpet woven with a weft-wrapping technique in which weft is wrapped around the warps, passing over four, under two, and over four in sequence.

Spandrel. The portion of a prayer rug that appears above and on either side of the mihrab, or the corner design of a rug field.

Spinning. Forming of a continuous strand of yarn by twisting fibers together by rotation, either with a drop spindle or a rod attached to a rotating or spinning wheel.

Swastika. Chinese symbol for luck.

Tagma. Tribal emblem occasionally woven into Turkish carpets.

Talim. Paper on which the design of a carpet has been written out, knot by knot. *See* Cartoon.

Tchuval. *See* Chuval.

Torba. Storage bag.

Turbehlik. Carpet woven in Turkey to be spread over a grave, the combined handiwork of members of the household as an expression of sorrow.

Turkish knot. Symmetrical or Ghiordes knot; a strand of yarn encircles two warp threads, with the loose ends drawn tightly between the two.

Turkoman. Refers to rugs from the Turkestan region. Their patterns are made up of repeated guls (geometric motifs) that were woven unique to each tribe.

Verneh. A flat weave created by an extra weft wrapping on a plain weave. This type of weave is used for floor coverings, animal covers, and storage bags.

Warp. Threads running longitudinally through the carpet and attached to the loom during the weaving process. It is on the warp threads that the knots are tied.

Weave pattern. The appearance of the weave from the back of the rug, including visibility and irregularities of the knot backs (nodes), warps, and wefts, and any repeated features that might be characteristic of a group.

Weft. Threads running perpendicular to the warp (left to right), used to secure the knots in place during the weaving process.

Yastik. Turkish term for small rugs or mats measuring approximately 18 by 39 inches (50 by 100 centimeters).

Yuruk. Name loosely applied to the numerous nomadic tribes residing throughout the Anatolian plateau.

Zaronim. Persian term for rugs measuring 39 by 60 inches (100 by 150 centimeters).

Zarquart. Persian term for rugs measuring approximately 27 by 54 inches (70 by 140 centimeters).

Zili. Pileless rug-weaving technique in which an extra weft floats on a plain weave. The extra floats split pairs of warps and are laid over and under the warps, so that the surface of the weave is completely covered with floats of two, three, or five warps.

Zil-i-Sultan. Vase of roses design, usually repeated in rows throughout the field of the carpet.

FOR FURTHER READING

Recommended sources for specific aspects of Oriental rugs are keyed as follows:

CA	CAUCASUS
CH	CHINA AND EASTERN TURKESTAN
G	GENERAL
IN	INDIA
IR	IRAN
P	PILELESS RUGS AND FLATWEAVES

R	REPAIR
TI	TIBET AND NEPAL
TR	TRIBAL
TU	TURKOMAN
TY	TURKEY

BOOKS AND ARTICLES

ALGROVE, J. *The Qashqa'i of Iran: The World of Islam Festival.* London: Whitworth Art Gallery, 1976. IR

ALLANE, LEE. *Chinese Rugs.* London: Thames & Hudson, 1992. CH

BECK, LOIS. *The Qashqa'i People of Southern Iran.* Los Angeles: UCLA Museum of Cultural History, 1981. TR

BEDOUKIAN, H. "Natural Dyes in Caucasian Rugs." *Oriental Rug Review* II:7 (October 1982).

BENNETT, IAN. *Oriental Rugs. Vol. 1, Caucasian.* London: Oriental Textile Press, 1980. CA

———, ed. *Rugs and Carpets of the World.* New York: A & W, 1977. G

BIDDER, HANS. *Carpets from Eastern Turkestan.* Accokeek, Ma.: Washington International Associates, 1979. CH

BIGGS, ROBERT, ed. *Discoveries from Kurdish Looms.* Chicago: Northwestern University Press, 1983. TR, IR, TY

BLACK, DAVID, ed. *The Macmillan Atlas of Rugs & Carpets.* New York: Macmillan, 1985.

———, and C. Loveless. *Rugs of the Wandering Balouchi.* London: David Black Oriental Carpets, 1967. TR

BOUCHER, JEFF. *Balouchi Woven Treasures.* Alexandria, Va.: Jeff W. Boucher, 1989. TR

CRAYCRAFT, M. *Belouch Prayer Rugs.* Pointe Reyes Station, Calif.: Dennis Anderson, 1982. TR

DHALL, D.P. and T.Z. "Rugs of the Afghanistan Balouchi." *Hali* V: 4 (1983).

DIAMOND, M. *Oriental Rugs in the Metropolitan Museum of Art.* New York: Metropolitan Museum of Art, 1973. G

EAGLETON, WILLIAM. *Kurdish Rugs.* New York: Interlink, 1988. TR

EDWARDS, CECIL. *The Persian Carpet.* London: Duckworth, 1953. IR

EILAND, MURRAY. *Oriental Rugs.* Boston: New York Graphic Society, 1976. G

FASAI, M.S. *Woven with Love: Tribal Gabbehs and Carpets from Fars.* Tehran: Negar Books, 1992.

FORD, P.R.J. *The Oriental Carpet.* New York: Abrams, 1981. G

GANS-REUDIN, E. *Chinese Carpets.* Tokyo: Kodansha International, 1981. CH

———. *Indian Carpets.* New York: Rizzoli, 1984. IN

———. *The Splendor of Persian Carpets.* New York: Rizzoli, 1978. IR

HERBERT, JANICE S. *Affordable Oriental Rugs.* New York: Macmillan, 1980. CH, IN, TI

———. *Oriental Rugs.* New York: Macmillan, 1982. G

HOUSEGO, J. *Tribal Rugs.* London: Scorpion, 1978. TR

ITEN-MARITZ, J. *Turkish Carpets.* Tokyo: Kodansha International, 1977. TY

ITTIG, ANNETTE. "A Group of Inscribed Carpets from Persian Kurdistan." *Hali* IV:2 (1981).

JUSTIN, VALERIE S. *Flat-Woven Rugs of the World.* New York: Van Nostrand Reinhold, 1980. P

LIPTON, MIMI. *The Tiger Rugs of Tibet.* London: Thames & Hudson, 1988. TI

LOGES, W. *Turkoman Tribal Rugs.* London: Allen & Unwin, 1980. TU

MACKIE, LOUISE, and J. THOMPSON, eds. *Turkomen.* Washington, D.C.: Textile Museum, 1980. TU

NEFF, IVAN. *Dictionary of Oriental Rugs.* London: Donker, 1974. G

O'BANNON, GEORGE. *The Turkoman Carpet.* London: Duckworth, 1974. TU

OPIE, JAMES. *Tribal Rugs.* Portland, Ore.: Tolstoy Press, 1992. TR

———. *Tribal Rugs of Southern Persia.* Portland, Ore.: James Opies Oriental Rugs, 1981. TR

PARSONS, R.D. *Oriental Rugs. Vol. 3, The Carpets of Afghanistan.* Woodbridge N.J.: Baron, 1983. TU

PETSOPOULOS, Y. *Kilims.* New York: Rizzoli, 1979. P

POZZA, NERI. *The Art of Dyeing.* Vicenza: Neri Possa Editore, 1973.

ROSTOV, CHARLES, and GUANYAN, JIA. *Chinese Carpets.* New York: Harry N. Abrams, 1983. CH

RYDER, M.L. *Sheep & Man.* London: Duckworth, 1983.

SABAHI, TAHER. *Splendeurs des Tapis D' Orient.* Paris: Groupe Editions Atlans, 1987.

SCHURMANN, ULRICH. *Caucasian Rugs.* Accokeek, Md.: Washington International Associates, 1964. CA

SMITH, M. "Levy Kelaty Talk on Modern Caucasian Rugs." *Hali* VI:3 (1984).

STONE, PETER. *Oriental Rug Repair.* Chicago: Greenleaf, 1981. R

———. *Rugs of the Caucasus: Structure and Design.* Chicago: Greenleaf, 1984. CA

TANAVOLI, PARVIZ and S. AMANOLAHI. *Gabbeh: The Georges D. Bornet Collection, Part 2.* Baar, Switzerland: Georges Bornet, n.d. TR

TANAVOLI, PARVIZ. *Shahsavan.* New York: Rizzoli, 1985.

THOMPSON, JON. *Oriental Carpets.* New York: Dutton, 1988. G

WARE, JOYCE. *The Official Price Guide: Oriental Rugs.* New York: House of Collectables, 1992. G

WRIGHT, RICHARD. *Rugs and Flatweaves of the Transcaucasus.* Pittsburgh: Pittsburgh Rug Society, 1980. CA

PERIODICALS

The Decorative Rug. Monthly. Editor R. O'Callaghan. For subscriptions, write to Oriental Rug Review, P.O. Box 709, Meredith, NH 03253.

Hali. Quarterly. Publisher and editor Alan Marcuson. For subscriptions in the U.S. and Canada, write to Hali Publications, c/o I.M.D. Ltd., LUVS Container Station, 149–05 177th Street, Jamaica, NY 11434. For other countries, contact Hali Publications Ltd., Kingsgate House, Kingsgate Place, London NW6 4TA, U.K.

Oriental Rug Magazine. Published quarterly by the Oriental Rug Importers Association. To the trade only. Write to ORIA, Inc., 267 Fifth Avenue, #302, New York, NY 10016.

Oriental Rug Review. Bimonthly. Covering Oriental rugs and other textiles. Editor R. O'Callaghan. Subscription requests to Oriental Rug Review, P.O. Box 709, Meredith, NH 03253.

Rug News. Monthly. Editor L. Stroh. To subscribe, write Museum Books, Inc., 6 West 37th Street, New York, NY 10018.

Summary of Rug Characteristics

Rugs are indexed according to their relative durability and price on a scale of 1 to 5, with 1 being the most durable and the most expensive and 5 being the least durable and the lowest price.

If rugs are commonly available new, old, and antique, they are marked as N (new), O (old), and A (antique). The average knot counts are given as well as the sizes most frequently encountered. For example, Bijar rugs are very durable and are generally expensive. New, old, and antique Bijar rugs are available. Bijars have an average knot count of 251 to 350 knots per square inch and are found in virtually all sizes.

| | Durability | Price | Antique, New, Old | Typical Knot Count | | | | | Common Sizes | | | | | |
				50–150	151–250	251–350	351–450	450+	2' x 4' or smaller	3' x 5' to 4' x 6'	5' x 8' to 6' x 9'	8' x 10' to 9' x 12'	10' x 14' or larger	Runners
Iran														
Abadeh	3	3	N		X				X	X	X			X
Afshar	4	4	AON	X	X					X	X			
Arak	3	3	AO	X	X							X	X	
Ardebil	3	3	N	X					X	X	X	X	X	X
Bakhtiari	2–4	2–4	AON	X	X	X				X	X	X	X	
Balouchi	4–5	4–5	AON	X					X	X				
Bijar	1	1	AON			X			X	X	X	X	X	
Birjand	3	4	N	X						X	X	X		
Bownat	3	2	N	X						X	X			
Dergazine	2–3	3	AON		X				X	X	X	X	X	X
Feraghan	2–3	2	AO	X	X				X	X				X
Gabbeh	2–4	2–3	ON	X					X	X	X			
Hamadan	2	3	AON	X	X				X	X	X	X		X
Herez	2–3	3–4	AON	X	X	X						X	X	X
Ingeles	2	3	ON	X					X	X				X
Isfahan	1–2	1	ON				X	X	X	X	X	X	X	
Joshaghan	2–4	3	ON		X	X			X	X	X	X		
Karaja	2	3	AON	X					X	X				X
Kashan	1–2	1–3	AON			X	X		X	X	X	X	X	X
Kelardasht	2–3	3	N	X					X	X	X			
Kerman	1	1–2	AON		X	X			X	X	X	X	X	X
Kolyai	3–4	3–4	ON	X					X	X		X		
Kurd	2–4	3–4	AON	X	X				X	X	X			X
Lillihan	2	3	AO	X	X				X	X				
Luri	3	2	AON	X						X	X			

	DURABILITY	PRICE	ANTIQUE, NEW, OLD	Typical Knot Count					Common Sizes					
				50–150	151–250	251–350	351–450	450+	2' X 4' OR SMALLER	3' X 5' TO 4' X 6'	5' X 8' TO 6' X 9'	8' X 10' TO 9' X 12'	10' X 14' OR LARGER	RUNNERS
Malayer	2	3	AON	X	X					X	X	X		
Mashad	2–3	2–3	AON	X	X					X	X	X	X	
Maslaghan	2	3	AON	X	X					X	X			
Meshkin	3–4	3–4	N	X						X	X	X	X	
Mud	3	3–4	N		X	X				X	X	X	X	
Nain	1–3	1–3	N			X	X		X	X	X	X	X	
Qashqa'i	3	3	AON		X				X	X	X			
Quchan	4	4	N	X						X				
Qum wool	1–2	1–2	N		X	X			X	X	X	X		
Qum silk	3	1–2	N				X	X	X	X	X	X		
Rudbar	3	3	N		X									X
Sarouk	1	1	AON			X			X	X	X	X	X	X
Senna	1–2	1–2	AON		X	X	X			X				
Serab	2	3	O		X									X
Seraband	2	2	AO	X	X	X					X	X	X	
Serapi	3	1	A		X	X						X	X	
Shiraz	3–5	3–5	AON	X						X	X	X		
Tabriz	1–4	1–4	AON	X	X	X	X		X	X	X	X	X	X
Tafresh	3	3	N	X	X				X	X				X
Veramin	1	2	ON		X	X				X	X	X		
Viss	3	4	N	X	X				X	X	X	X		
Yelemeh	2–3	2–3	N	X	X				X	X	X	X		
Yezd	2	2	ON		X							X	X	
CAUCASUS														
Akstafa	3	2	AO	X										X
Baku	3	2	AO	X						X				
Gendge	3	2	AO	X						X				X
Karabagh	3	2–3	AO	X						X	X			X
Kazak	3	1–2	AO	X					X	X	X			X
Kuba	2–3	2	AO	X					X	X				X
Shirvan	3	2–3	AO	X					X	X				X
Talish	3	2	AO	X						X				X
Modern Caucasian	2–3	3	N	X	X				X	X	X	X		

	Durability	Price	Antique, New, Old	Typical Knot Count					Common Sizes					
				50–150	151–250	251–350	351–450	450+	2' x 4' or smaller	3' x 5' to 4' x 6'	5' x 8' to 6' x 9'	8' x 10' to 9' x 12'	10' x 14' or larger	Runners
TURKESTAN AND AFGHANISTAN														
Chodor	3	2	AO	X							X			
Daulatabad	2	3	N	X					X	X	X	X	X	X
Ersari	3–4	3–4	AON	X					X	X	X	X	X	
Mauri	2-3	2–3	N		X				X	X	X	X	X	X
Salor	3	1	AO			X					X	X		
Sariq	3	3	AO	X							X		X	
Tekke	3	3	AON	X					X	X	X	X		
Yomud	3	3	AON	X							X	X		
TURKEY														
Ayvacik	4	4	ON	X						X				
Bergama	3	2	AON		X				X	X				
Demirci	4	2	AO	X						X				
DOBAG	3	3	N	X					X	X	X			
Dosemealti	4	4	N	X						X				
Ezine	4	3–4	ON	X						X				
Hereke														
wool	1	1	N		X	X					X	X		
silk	3	1	ON			X	X		X	X	X			
Kars	3	4	ON	X						X	X			
Kayseri														
wool	4	4	ON	X	X	X			X	X	X	X	X	
"art" silk	4	4	N	X	X				X	X	X			
Kirshehir	4	2	AON	X						X				
Konya	3–4	2–3	AON	X					X	X				
Kozak	3–4	3	ON	X					X	X				
Kula	3	3	AON	X					X	X	X			
Ladik	3	2	AON	X					X	X				
Melas	4	3–4	AON	X						X				
Mudjar	4	2	AO	X					X	X				
Ushak	3–5	2	AON	X									X	X
Yagcibecir	4–5	4–5	N	X					X	X				

	Durability	Price	Antique, New, Old	Typical Knot Count					Common Sizes					
				50–150	151–250	251–350	351–450	450+	2' X 4' or smaller	3' X 5' to 4' X 6'	5' X 8' to 6' X 9'	8' X 10' to 9' X 12'	10' X 14' or larger	Runners
China and Eastern Turkestan														
Baotou	3	3	AO	X					X	X				
Beijing	4	3	O	X								X	X	
Gansu	3	3	AO	X					X	X				
Modern Chinese														
wool	2–3	2–4	N	X	X				X	X	X	X	X	X
silk	3	3	N	X	X	X			X	X	X			
Ningxia	3	3	AO	X					X	X				
Tientsin	3	3	O	X					X	X		X	X	X
Tibet and Nepal														
Xingiang	3–4	2–4	AON	X					X	X	X	X	X	
Nepalese	2	3–4	N	X					X	X	X	X		X
Tibetan	2–4	2–4	AON	X					X	X	X			
India														
Agra	3–4	3–4	ON	X	X				X	X	X	X	X	
Jaipur	3–4	3–4	ON	X	X				X	X	X	X	X	
Kashmir wool	3	3	ON	X	X	X			X	X	X	X		
Kashmir silk	3	3	N		X	X			X	X	X	X		
Mirzapur Badohi	3–5	3–5	ON	X					X	X	X	X	X	X
Pakistan														
Bukhara	3–4	3–5	N	X	X	X			X	X	X	X	X	X
Persian design	2–3	2–3	N		X	X			X	X	X	X	X	X
Romania														
Braila	3	3	N	X					X	X	X	X	X	X
Brasov	3	3	N	X						X	X			
Bucharesti	3	4	N	X					X	X	X	X	X	X
Harman	3	3	N	X							X	X	X	X
Milcov	2	2	N		X					X				
Mures	2	2	N	X								X	X	
Olt	4	3	N	X								X	X	
Transylvania	3	3	N	X						X	X	X		X

INDEX